Microsoft® Official Academic Course

LAB MANUAL

Materials Excerpted from

Windows Server® 2008
Active Directory® Configuration
Microsoft Certified Technology Specialist Exam 70-640
Lab Manual

Windows Server® 2008
Network Infrastructure Configuration
Microsoft Certified Technology Specialist Exam 70-642
Lab Manual

Windows Server® 2008
Administrator
Microsoft Certified IT Professional Exam 70-646
Lab Manual

LEARNING SOLUTIONS

To order books or for customer service, please call 1(800)-CALL-WILEY (225-5945).

Printed in the United States of America.

ISBN 978- 0-470-87733-3

Printed and bound by Bind-Rite Graphics, Inc.

10 9 8 7 6 5 4 3 2 1

The content of this lab manual has been taken from

Microsoft® Official Academic Course
Windows Server® 2008
Active Directory® Configuration
Microsoft Certified Technology Specialist Exam 70-640
Lab Manual

Microsoft® Official Academic Course
Windows Server® 2008
Network Infrastructure Configuration
Microsoft Certified Technology Specialist Exam 70-642
Lab Manual

And

Microsoft® Official Academic Course
Windows Server® 2008
Administrator
Microsoft Certified IT Professional Exam 70-646
Lab Manual

Since this custom lab manual is based on excerpts of the full Microsoft® Official Academic Course lab manuals for 70-640, 70-642, and 70-646, it is not intended to cover the entire objective domain for these three Microsoft® certification exams. In that way, this custom lab manual is not meant to be a preparatory lab manual for these three Microsoft® certification exams.

EXECUTIVE EDITOR	John Kane
EDITORIAL ASSISTANT	Jennifer Lartz
DIRECTOR OF MARKETING AND SALES	Mitchell Beaton
PRODUCTION MANAGER	Micheline Frederick
PRODUCTION EDITOR	Kerry Weinstein
DEVELOPMENT AND PRODUCTION	Custom Editorial Productions, Inc.

To order books or for customer service, please call 1-800-CALL WILEY (225-5945).

ISBN   978-0-470-22508-0 (70-640 Lab)
        978-0-470-22514-1 (70-642 Lab)
        978-0-470-22510-3 (70-646 Lab)

Printed in the United States of America

10 9 8 7 6 5 4 3 2 1

BRIEF CONTENTS

CONTENTS

LAB 1.1
INSTALLING MICROSOFT WINDOWS SERVER 2008

This lab contains the following exercises and activities:

Exercise 1.1.1   Installing Windows Server 2008

Exercise 1.1.2   Configuring Windows Server 2008

Exercise 1.1.3   Installing and Configuring a Second Windows Server 2008 Computer

Exercise 1.1.4   Installing and Configuring a Windows Server 2008 Server Core Computer (optional)

Exercise 1.1.5   Installing and Configuring a Windows Vista Computer (optional)

Lab Review   Questions

Lab Challenge   Joining an Active Directory Domain

BEFORE YOU BEGIN

Lab 1.1 assumes that setup has been completed as specified in the setup document and that your computer has connectivity to other lab computers and the Internet.

For subsequent labs, mandatory exercises require the use of two (2) Windows Server 2008 Enterprise Edition servers. Additionally, optional exercises are provided that involve a server running Windows Server 2008 Server Core and a workstation running Windows Vista Enterprise Edition. You can use multiple physical computers, or you can use Microsoft Virtual PC or Virtual Server to install and run multiple servers on a single machine. This manual assumes you are using multiple virtual machines under Microsoft Virtual PC. In the optional exercises for this lab, Exercises 1.1.4 and 1.1.5, you will perform the prerequisite configuration of the Server Core and Vista computers necessary to perform the optional exercises in future lessons.

The instructor PC is preconfigured as a domain controller in the lucernepublishing.com domain for demonstration purposes and is named INSTRUCTOR01.

> **NOTE**
>
> *In this lab manual, you will see the characters xx, yy, and zz. These directions assume that you are working on computers configured in pairs and that each computer has a number. One number is odd, and the other number is even. For example, W2K801 is the odd-numbered computer, and W2K802 is the even-numbered computer. When you see xx, substitute the unique number assigned to the odd-numbered computer. When you see yy, substitute the unique number assigned to the even-numbered computer. When you see zz, substitute the number assigned to the computer that you are working at, either odd or even.*

The four Windows Server 2008 server computers referenced in this lab will each be configured with static IP addresses. For ease of reference, record the static IP addresses of each server that you will be working with in this lab:

INSTRUCTOR01 (Instructor Computer)

IP Address: ___.___.___.___

Subnet Mask: ___.___.___.___

Default Gateway: ___.___.___.___

W2K8*xx*: (For example: W2K801)

IP Address: ___.___.___.___

Subnet Mask: ___.___.___.___

Default Gateway: ___.___.___.___

W2K8*yy*: (For example: W2K802)

IP Address: ___.___.___.___

Subnet Mask: ___.___.___.___

Default Gateway: ___.___.___.___

CORE*xx*: (For example: CORE01)

IP Address: ___.___.___.___

Subnet Mask: ___.___.___.___

Default Gateway: ___.___.___.___

SCENARIO

You are a network support specialist for Lucerne Publishing. Lucerne Publishing has implemented the lucernepublishing.com Active Directory forest as a single-domain environment. After preparing several pre-installed Windows Server 2008 servers to be deployed as file servers, DNS servers, and other infrastructure servers in remote offices, you are informed by IT management that several new offices are about to open that will also require new servers to be installed.

After completing this lab, you will be able to:

- Install and configure the Windows Server 2008 operating system

- (Optional) Install and configure a Server Core computer

- (Optional) Install and configure a Windows Vista workstation

Estimated lab time: 155 minutes

Exercise 1.1.1	Installing Windows Server 2008
Overview	You have just procured a new machine on which you now need to install the Windows Server 2008 operating system. You have the Windows Server 2008 installation media available.
Outcomes	After completing this exercise, you will know how to: ▲ Install the Windows Server 2008 operating system
Completion time	20 minutes
Precautions	N/A

1. Either insert the Windows Server 2008 media into the appropriate disk drive on the odd-numbered computer, or configure the virtual machine to use an ISO file as indicated by your lab instructor or proctor. Reboot the Windows Server 2008 server or virtual machine. The Install Windows screen appears.

Question 1	*What drop-down boxes are available on the initial installation screen?*

2. Select the appropriate values for the Language to Install, Time and Currency Format, and Keyboard or Input Method drop-down boxes as provided by your instructor or lab proctor. Click Next, and then click Install now.

3. The Select the operating system you want to install screen appears. Select Windows Server 2008 Enterprise (Full Installation), and then click Next.

4. The Please Read the License Terms screen appears. Read the terms of the Windows Server 2008 license agreement, place a checkmark next to I accept the license terms, and then click Next.

5. The Which Type of Installation Do You Want? screen appears.

Question 2	*Why is the Upgrade option disabled?*

6. Click the Custom (advanced) selection. The Where do you want to install Windows? screen appears. Accept the default selection, and click Next.

7. The Installing Windows screen appears. Allow the installation to progress; the computer will reboot multiple times during the process.

8. After the final reboot, you will be prompted to set an initial password for the operating system installation. Click OK. Enter **MSPress#1** as the local Administrator password, and then re-enter the password to confirm.

9. Click the blue arrow to set the initial password, and then click OK.

NOTE	*If you are working with virtualization software, such as Virtual PC, you should now install any software extensions that come with the virtual software to improve the performance of the virtual machine.*

Exercise 1.1.2	Configuring Windows Server 2008
Overview	You have just installed a new Windows Server 2008 computer using the default installation settings. You need to modify some basic settings on the server before you can configure it as an infrastructure server.
Outcomes	After completing this exercise, you will know how to: ▲ Log on to a Windows Server 2008 computer ▲ Explore the Initial Configuration Tasks interface ▲ Modify basic settings on a Windows Server 2008 computer ▲ Configure network settings on a Windows Server 2008 computer
Completion time	20 minutes
Precautions	The instructions presume that the lab environment has been configured using the 192.168.1.0/24 Class C address range, with addresses 192.168.1.100–192.168.1.130 reserved for assigning static IP addresses to student computers. If your lab environment uses a different IP addressing scheme, your instructor or lab proctor will provide the appropriate IP addressing values.

■ PART A: CONFIGURING BASIC SETTINGS ON A WINDOWS SERVER 2008 COMPUTER

1. Press Ctrl+Alt+Delete on the newly installed computer, and log on as the default administrator of the local computer. Your username is Administrator. The password is MSPress#1 or the password that your instructor or lab proctor assigns to you. The Initial Configuration Tasks (ICT) window will be displayed automatically.

2. Expand the ICT window to fill the screen if necessary.

3. Click Set time zone. The Date and Time window will be displayed.

4. Click Change time zone. The Time zone settings window will be displayed.

5. In the Time zone drop-down box, select the appropriate time zone, and click OK. You will return to the Date and Time window.

6. Click OK to return to the ICT window.

7. Click Enable automatic updating and feedback. The Enable Windows Automated Updating and Feedback window opens. Click Enable Windows automatic updating and feedback (recommended).

8. Click Provide computer name and domain. The System Properties window will be displayed.

9. On the Computer Name tab, click Change. The Computer Name/Domain Changes window is displayed.

10. In the Computer name text box, key **W2K8xx** for your computer name, where *xx* corresponds to the odd-numbered computer that your instructor or lab proctor has assigned to you. Click OK. A Computer Name/Domain Changes dialog box is displayed, informing you that you must restart your computer to apply these changes. Click OK to acknowledge this dialog box.

11. Click Close to close the System Properties window. You will be prompted to restart your computer to apply the name change. Click Restart Now. Your Windows Server 2008 computer will restart.

■ PART B: CONFIGURING TCP/IP SETTINGS ON A WINDOWS SERVER 2008 COMPUTER

1. Press Ctrl+Alt+Delete on the W2K8*xx* computer, and log on as the default administrator of the local computer. Your username will be Administrator. The password will be MSPress#1 or the password that your instructor or lab proctor assigns to you. The ICT window will be displayed automatically.

2. Place a checkmark next to Do not show this window at logon. Click Close to close the ICT window. The Server Manager window is displayed automatically. Expand the Server Manager window to fill the screen if necessary.

3. Click View Network Connections. The Network Connections window is displayed.

4. Right-click your network connection, and select Properties. The network connection's Properties window will be displayed.

Question 3	*What network components are installed on your computer?*

5. Click Internet Protocol Version 4 (TCP/IPv4), and select Properties. The Internet Protocol Version 4 (TCP/IPv4) Properties window will be displayed.

6. Select the Use the following IP address: radio button. Enter the following IP address information for the instructor computer that you recorded at the beginning of this lab.

IP Address: for example, 192.168.1.101

Subnet Mask: for example, 255.255.255.0

Default Gateway: for example, 192.168.1.1

7.   Click OK, and then click Close to save your changes. Close the Network Connections window.

8.   Log off of the W2K8*xx* computer.

Exercise 1.1.3	Installing and Configuring a Second Windows Server 2008 Computer
Overview	Your manager assigned to you the task of installing and configuring an additional Windows Server 2008 computer to function as an infrastructure server in one of your branch offices. To begin, you must install the operating system on this server, after which you must set up this computer with basic configuration information and static IP address settings.
Outcomes	After completing this exercise, you will know how to: ▲ Log on to a Windows Server 2008 computer ▲ Explore the Initial Configuration Tasks interface ▲ Modify basic settings on a Windows Server 2008 computer ▲ Configure network settings on a Windows Server 2008 computer
Completion time	25 minutes
Precautions	N/A

■ PART A: INSTALLING THE WINDOWS SERVER 2008 OPERATING SYSTEM ON A SECOND COMPUTER

1.   Either insert the Windows Server 2008 media into the appropriate disk drive on the even-numbered computer, or configure the virtual machine to use an ISO file as indicated by your lab instructor or proctor. Reboot the Windows Server 2008 server or virtual machine. The Install Windows screen appears.

2.   Select the appropriate values for the Language to Install, Time and Currency Format, and Keyboard or Input Method drop-down boxes as provided by your instructor or lab proctor. Click Next, and then click Install now.

3.   The Select the operating system you want to install screen appears. Select Windows Server 2008 Enterprise (Full Installation), and then click Next.

4. The Please read the license terms screen appears. Read the terms of the Windows Server 2008 license agreement, place a checkmark next to I accept the license terms, and then click Next.

5. The Which type of installation do you want? screen appears.

6. Click the Custom (advanced) selection. The Where do you want to install Windows? screen appears. Accept the default selection, and click Next.

7. The Installing Windows screen appears. Allow the installation to progress; the computer will reboot multiple times during the process.

8. After the final reboot, you will be prompted to set an initial password for the operating system installation. Click OK. Enter **MSPress#1** as the local Administrator password, and then re-enter the password to confirm.

9. Click the blue arrow to set the initial password, and then click OK.

> **NOTE** *If you are working with virtualization software, such as Virtual PC, you should now install any software extensions that come with the virtual software to improve the performance of the virtual machine.*

■ PART B: CONFIGURING BASIC SETTINGS ON THE SECOND WINDOWS SERVER 2008 COMPUTER

1. Press Ctrl+Alt+Delete on the newly installed second computer assigned to you, and log on as the default administrator of the local computer. Your username will be Administrator. The password will be MSPress#1 or the password that your instructor or lab proctor assigns to you. The Initial Configuration Tasks (ICT) window will be displayed automatically. Expand the ICT window to fill the full screen if necessary.

2. Click Set time zone. The Date and Time window will be displayed.

3. Click Change time zone. The Time zone settings window will be displayed.

4. In the Time zone drop-down box, select the appropriate time zone, and click OK. You will return to the Date and Time window.

5. Click OK to return to the ICT window.

6. Click Enable automatic updating and feedback. Click Enable Windows automatic updating and feedback (recommended).

7. Click Provide computer name and domain. The System Properties window will be displayed.

Question 4	*What is the current name of your computer?*

8. On the Computer Name tab, click Change. The Computer Name/Domain Changes window will appear.

9. In the Computer name text box, enter **W2K8**yy for your computer name, where yy corresponds to the even-numbered computer that your instructor or lab proctor has assigned to you. Click OK. A Computer Name/Domain Changes dialog box will be displayed, informing you that you must restart your computer to apply these changes. Click OK to acknowledge this dialog box.

10. Click Close to close the System Properties window. You will be prompted to restart your computer to apply the name change. Click Restart Now. Your Windows Server 2008 computer will restart.

■ PART C: CONFIGURING A STATIC IP ADDRESS ON THE SECOND WINDOWS SERVER 2008 COMPUTER

1. Press Ctrl+Alt+Delete on the W2K8yy server, and log on as the default administrator of the local computer. Your username will be Administrator. The password will be MSPress#1 or the password that your instructor or lab proctor assigns to you. The Initial Configuration Tasks (ICT) window will be displayed automatically.

2. Place a checkmark next to Do not show this window at logon. Click Close to close the ICT window. The Server Manager screen will be displayed automatically. Expand the Server Manager window to fit the full screen if necessary.

Question 5	*What is the current name of your computer?*

3. Click View Network Connections. The Network Connections window will be displayed.

4. Right-click your network connection, and select Properties. The network connection's Properties window will be displayed.

5. Click Internet Protocol Version 4 (TCP/IPv4), and select Properties. The Internet Protocol Version 4 (TCP/IPv4) Properties window will be displayed.

6. Select the Use the following IP address radio button. Enter the following IP address information for the Read-Only DC that you recorded at the beginning of this lab.

    IP Address: for example, 192.168.1.102

    Subnet Mask: for example, 255.255.255.0

    Default Gateway: for example, 192.168.1.1

7. Click OK, and then click Close to save your changes. Close the Network Connections window.

8. Log off of the W2K8*yy* server.

Exercise 1.1.4 (optional)	Installing and Configuring a Windows Server 2008 Server Core Computer
Overview	Your manager assigned to you the task of preparing an additional Windows Server 2008 computer running Server Core to function as an infrastructure server in one of your branch offices. To begin, you must install and configure this third Windows Server 2008 computer with basic configuration information and static IP address settings. Because this server is running the Server Core installation option, you must perform most of the configuration from the command line.
Outcomes	After completing this exercise, you will know how to: ▲ Install the Windows Server 2008 Server Core operating system installation option ▲ Log on to a Windows Server 2008 Server Core computer ▲ Modify basic settings on a Windows Server 2008 Server Core computer ▲ Configure network settings on a Windows Server 2008 Server Core computer ▲ Enable remote administration exceptions in the Windows Firewall of a Server Core computer
Completion time	30 minutes
Precautions	N/A

■ **PART A: INSTALLING WINDOWS SERVER 2008 SERVER CORE**

1. Either insert the Windows Server 2008 media into the appropriate disk drive, or configure the virtual machine to use an ISO file as indicated by your lab

instructor or proctor. Reboot the Windows Server 2008 server or virtual machine. The Install Windows screen appears.

2. Select the appropriate values for the Language to Install, Time and Currency Format, and Keyboard or Input Method drop-down boxes as provided by your instructor or lab proctor. Click Next, and then click Install now.

3. The Select the operating system you want to install screen appears. Select Windows Server 2008 Enterprise (Server Core Installation), and then click Next.

4. The Please read the license terms screen appears. Read the terms of the Windows Server 2008 license agreement, place a checkmark next to I accept the license terms, and then click Next.

5. The Which type of installation do you want? screen appears.

6. Click the Custom (advanced) selection. The Where do you want to install Windows? screen appears. Accept the default selection, and click Next.

7. The Installing Windows screen appears. Allow the installation to progress; the computer will reboot multiple times during the process.

8. After the final reboot, you will be presented with an "Other User" login prompt. Log on as Administrator with a blank password, after which you will be prompted to set an initial password for the operating system installation. Click OK. Enter **MSPress#1** as the new local Administrator password, and then re-enter the password to confirm.

9. Click the blue arrow to set the initial password, and then click OK.

> **NOTE**
>
> *If you are working with virtualization software, such as Virtual PC, you should now install any software extensions that come with the virtual software to improve the performance of the virtual machine.*

■ PART B: CONFIGURING THE SERVER TIME ZONE AND COMPUTER NAME.

1. Press Ctrl+Alt+Delete on the third Windows Server 2008 computer assigned to you, and log on as the default administrator of the local computer. Your username will be Administrator. The password will be MSPress#1 or the password that your instructor or lab proctor assigns to you.

Question 6	*What do you see when you log on to a Server Core computer?*

2. Key **timedate.cpl** at the command prompt, and press Enter. The Date and Time window is displayed.

3. Click Change time zone. The Time zone settings window will be displayed.

4. In the Time zone drop-down box, select the appropriate time zone, and click OK. You will return to the Date and Time window. Click OK to return to the command prompt.

5. Key **hostname** at the command prompt, and press Enter.

6. Key **netdom /?**, at the command prompt, and press Enter.

7. At the command prompt, key **netdom renamecomputer %computername% /newname:CORExx**, and press Enter.

8. Key **y**, and then press Enter.

9. Key **shutdown /r** at the command prompt, and press Enter. A pop-up window informs you that Windows will shut down in less than a minute. Click Close, and allow the computer to restart.

■ PART C: CONFIGURING A STATIC IP ADDRESS.

1. Press Ctrl+Alt+Delete on CORExx, and log on as the default administrator of the local computer. Your username will be Administrator. The password will be MSPress#1 or the password that your instructor or lab proctor assigns to you.

2. Key **ipconfig /all** at the command prompt, and press Enter.

3. Key **netsh**, and then press Enter. Key **?**, and press Enter.

4. Key **interface**, and then press Enter. Key **?**, and press Enter.

5. Key **ipv4**, and then press Enter. Key **?**, and press Enter.

6. Key **set address name="Local Area Connection" source=static address=<IP Address> mask=<Subnet Mask> gateway=<Default Gateway> gwmetric=1**. Press Enter to assign the appropriate static IP configuration as recorded at the beginning of Lab 2. Key **exit** to return to the command prompt.

7. Key **ipconfig /all**, and press Enter.

8. Log off of the CORE*xx* computer.

■ PART D: ENABLING REMOTE ADMINISTRATION OF THE SERVER CORE COMPUTER

1. Press Ctrl+Alt+Delete on CORE*xx*, and log on as the default administrator of the local computer. Your username will be Administrator. The password will be MSPress#1 or the password that your instructor or lab proctor assigns to you.

2. At the command prompt, key **netsh advfirewall set allprofiles settings remotemanagement enable** to allow remote access to the server via the Computer Management MMC, the C$ shares, and so forth, and then press Enter.

3. At the command prompt, key **shutdown /l**, and then press Enter to log off of the computer.

Exercise 1.1.5 (optional)	Installing and Configuring a Windows Vista Computer
Overview	Your manager assigned to you the task of preparing Windows Vista workstations to be deployed to your branch offices. You must install and configure the Windows Vista operating system to create a consistent image for use in large-scale workstation deployments.
Outcomes	After completing this exercise, you will know how to: ▲ Install the Windows Vista operating system ▲ Log on to a Windows Vista computer ▲ Modify basic settings on a Windows Vista computer ▲ Configure network settings on a Windows Vista computer
Completion time	30 minutes
Precautions	N/A

1. Either insert the Windows Vista Ultimate media into the appropriate disk drive, or configure the virtual machine to use an ISO file as indicated by your lab instructor or proctor. Reboot the Windows Vista workstation or virtual machine. The Install Windows screen appears.

2. Select the appropriate values for the Language to Install, Time and Currency Format, and Keyboard or Input Method drop-down boxes as provided by your instructor or lab proctor. Click Next, and then click Install now.

3. The Type your product key for activation screen appears. Enter a legitimate Windows Vista product key, and then click Next.

4. The Please read the license terms screen appears. Read the terms of the Windows Server 2008 license agreement, place a checkmark next to I accept the license terms, and then click Next.

5. The Which type of installation do you want? screen appears.

6. Click the Custom (advanced) selection. The Where do you want to install Windows? screen appears. Accept the default selection, and click Next.

7. The Installing Windows screen appears. Allow the installation to progress; the computer will reboot multiple times during the process.

8. After the final installation reboot, the Choose a user name and picture screen will appear. In the Type a user name field, enter **STUDENT*xx***, where *xx* corresponds to the student number that was assigned by your instructor or lab proctor. In the Type a password field and the Retype your password field, enter **MSPress#1**. In the Type a password hint field, enter **"70-642 Lab Default"**. Click Next.

9. The Type a computer name and choose a desktop background screen appears. Enter **VISTA*xx*** as the computer name, and then click Next.

10. The Help protect windows automatically screen appears. Click Use recommended settings.

11. The Review your time and date settings screen appears. Enter the appropriate time zone and the current time. Click Next and then Start. If you are prompted for a network location, select Work.

12. Log off of the VISTA*xx* computer.

> **NOTE** *If you are working with virtualization software, such as Virtual PC, you should now install any software extensions that come with the virtual software to improve the performance of the virtual machine.*

LAB REVIEW QUESTIONS

Completion time	15 minutes

1. In your own words, describe what you learned by completing this lab.

2. What is the difference between a Full Installation of Windows Server 2008 and installing Windows Server 2008 Server Core?

3. Explore the reg.exe Windows Server 2008 command-line help by keying **reg /?**. Record three commands that you can issue from the command line using the reg utility, and describe what each command does:

LAB CHALLENGE: JOINING AN ACTIVE DIRECTORY DOMAIN

Completion time	15 minutes

You have completed the installation of several Windows Server 2008 and Windows Vista computers on your network. To test several configuration items that are dependent on Active Directory, you wish to join these computers to the lucernepublishing.com Active Directory domain that is hosted on the INSTRUCTOR01 Windows Server 2008 computer.

After completing this exercise, you will know how to:

▲ Join an Active Directory domain

Join each computer in this lab to the lucernepublishing.com Active Directory domain that is hosted on the INSTRUCTOR01 Windows Server 2008 computer. Either use LP\Administrator as the domain credentials to join each computer to the domain with a password of MSPress#1, or use the credentials provided by your instructor or lab proctor.

> **NOTE**
> *You will need to configure DNS on each computer to point to INSTRUCTOR01 as its preferred DNS server.*

When you are finished, drop each computer back into a workgroup configuration, and reverse any changes that you made to each computer's network configuration to allow the computer to join the Active Directory domain.

LAB 1.2
INTRODUCING WINDOWS SERVER 2008 NETWORKING

This lab contains the following exercises and activities:

Exercise 1.2.1   Modifying Basic Server Settings

Exercise 1.2.2   Configuring TCP/IP Settings

Exercise 1.2.3   Configuring a Second Windows Server 2008 Computer

Exercise 1.2.4   Configuring a Windows Server 2008 Server Core Computer (optional)

Lab Review   Questions

Lab Challenge   Configuring the Windows Firewall

BEFORE YOU BEGIN

Lab 1.2 assumes that setup has been completed as specified in the setup document and that your computer has connectivity to other lab computers and the Internet.

For subsequent labs, mandatory exercises require the use of two (2) Windows Server 2008 Enterprise Edition servers. Additionally, optional exercises are provided that involve a server running Windows Server 2008 Server Core and a workstation running Windows Vista Enterprise Edition. You can use multiple physical computers, or you can use Microsoft Virtual PC or Virtual Server to install and run multiple servers on a single machine.

The instructor PC is preconfigured as a domain controller in the lucernepublishing.com domain for demonstration purposes and is named INSTRUCTOR01.

> **NOTE**
>
> *In this lab manual, you will see the characters xx, yy, and zz. These directions assume that you are working on computers configured in pairs and that each computer has a number. One number is odd, and the other number is even. For example, W2K801 is the odd-numbered computer, and W2K802 is the even-numbered computer. When you see xx, substitute the unique number assigned to the odd-numbered computer. When you see yy, substitute the unique number assigned to the even-numbered computer. When you see zz, substitute the number assigned to the computer that you are working at, either odd or even.*

The three Windows Server 2008 server computers will be configured with static IP addresses. For ease of reference, record the static IP addresses of each server that you will be working with in this lab:

INSTRUCTOR01 (Instructor Computer)

IP Address: ___.___.___.___

Subnet Mask: ___.___.___.___

Default Gateway: ___.___.___.___

W2K8*xx*: (For example: W2K801)

IP Address: ___.___.___.___

Subnet Mask: ___.___.___.___

Default Gateway: ___.___.___.___

W2K8*yy*: (For example: W2K802)

IP Address: ___.___.___.___

Subnet Mask: ___.___.___.___

Default Gateway: ___.___.___.___

CORE*xx*: (For example: CORE01)

IP Address: ___.___.___.___

Subnet Mask: ___.___.___.___

Default Gateway: ___.___.___.___

SCENARIO

You are a network support specialist for Lucerne Publishing. Lucerne Publishing has implemented the lucernepublishing.com Active Directory forest as a single-domain environment. You are responsible for preparing several Windows Server 2008 servers to be deployed as file servers, DNS servers, and other infrastructure servers in remote offices. Because these servers were configured with only the default installation options, you have several tasks.

After completing this lab, you will be able to:

- Explore the Windows Server 2008 server interface to become familiar with its administration

- Modify basic settings on a Windows Server 2008 server

- Configure TCP/IP to prepare the Windows Server 2008 computer

- (Optional) Configure a Server Core computer

Estimated lab time: 100 minutes

Exercise 1.2.1	Modifying Basic Server Settings
Overview	You have just installed a new Windows Server 2008 computer using the default installation settings. You need to modify some basic settings on the server before you can configure it as an infrastructure server.
Outcomes	After completing this exercise, you will know how to: ▲ Log on to a Windows Server 2008 computer ▲ Explore the Initial Configuration Tasks interface ▲ Modify basic settings on a Windows Server 2008 computer
Completion time	10 minutes
Precautions	If you have completed Lab 1.1, you may skip this exercise because its steps are encompassed in Lab Exercise 1.1.2.

1. Press Ctrl+Alt+Delete on the odd-numbered computer, and log on as the default administrator of the local computer. Your username is Administrator. The password is MSPress#1 or the password that your instructor or lab proctor assigns to you. The Initial Configuration Tasks (ICT) window will display automatically.

2. Expand the ICT window to fill the screen if necessary.

Question 1	*What three categories of tasks are listed in the ICT interface?*

Question 2	*What is the current time zone configured for this computer?*

3. Click Set time zone. The Date and Time window will be displayed.

4. Click Change time zone. The Time zone settings window will be displayed.

5. In the Time zone drop-down box, select the appropriate time zone, and click OK. You will return to the Date and Time window.

Question 3	*Why does a shield icon appear next to the Change date and time button?*

6. Click OK to return to the ICT window.

7. Click Enable automatic updating and feedback. The Enable Windows Automated Updating and Feedback window opens. Click Enable Windows automatic updating and feedback (recommended).

8. Click Provide computer name and domain. The System Properties window will be displayed.

Question 4	*What is the current name of your computer?*

9. On the Computer Name tab, click Change. The Computer Name/Domain Changes window is displayed.

10. In the Computer name text box, key **W2K8xx** for your computer name, where *xx* corresponds to the odd-numbered computer that your instructor or lab proctor has assigned to you. Click OK. A Computer Name/Domain Changes dialog box is displayed, informing you that you must restart your computer to apply these changes. Click OK to acknowledge this dialog box.

11. Click Close to close the System Properties window. You will be prompted to restart your computer to apply the name change. Click Restart Now. Your Windows Server 2008 computer will restart.

Exercise 1.2.2	Configuring TCP/IP Settings
Overview	Your manager assigned to you the task of preparing a new Windows Server 2008 computer to function as an infrastructure server. To begin, you must configure this computer with static IP address settings.
Outcomes	After completing this exercise, you will know how to: ▲ Configure network settings on a Windows Server 2008 computer
Completion time	15 minutes
Precautions	1. The instructions presume that the lab environment has been configured using the 192.168.1.0/24 Class C address range, with addresses 192.168.1.100–192.168.1.130 reserved for assigning static IP addresses to student computers. If your lab environment uses a different IP addressing scheme, your instructor or lab proctor will provide the appropriate IP addressing values. 2. If you have completed Lab 1.1, you may skip this exercise because its steps are encompassed in Lab Exercise 1.1.2.

1. Press Ctrl+Alt+Delete on the W2K8*xx* computer, and log on as the default administrator of the local computer. Your username will be Administrator. The password will be MSPress#1 or the password that your instructor or lab proctor assigns to you. The Initial Configuration Tasks (ICT) window will be displayed automatically.

2. Place a checkmark next to Do not show this window at logon. Click Close to close the ICT window. The Server Manager window is displayed automatically. Expand the Server Manager window to fill the screen if necessary.

Question 5	*What name is assigned to your computer?*

3. Click View Network Connections. The Network Connections window is displayed.

NOTE	*You can also configure network settings from the ICT screen.*

4. Right-click your network connection, and select Properties. The network connection's Properties window will be displayed.

Question 6	*What network components are installed on your computer?*

5. Click Internet Protocol Version 4 (TCP/IPv4), and select Properties. The Internet Protocol Version 4 (TCP/IPv4) Properties window will be displayed.

Question 7	*What IP addressing settings are configured by default?*

6. Select the Use the following IP address: radio button. Enter the following IP address information for the odd-numbered computer that you recorded at the beginning of this lab.

   IP Address: for example, 192.168.1.101

   Subnet Mask: for example, 255.255.255.0

   Default Gateway: for example, 192.168.1.1

7. Click OK, and then click Close to save your changes. Close the Network Connections window.

8. Log off of the W2K8*xx* computer.

Exercise 1.2.3	Configuring a Second Windows Server 2008 Computer
Overview	Your manager assigned to you the task of preparing an additional Windows Server 2008 computer to function as an infrastructure server in one of your branch offices. To begin, you must set up this computer with basic configuration information and static IP address settings.
Outcomes	After completing this exercise, you will know how to: ▲ Log on to a Windows Server 2008 computer ▲ Explore the Initial Configuration Tasks interface ▲ Modify basic settings on a Windows Server 2008 computer ▲ Configure network settings on a Windows Server 2008 computer
Completion time	25 minutes
Precautions	If you have completed Lab 1.1, you may skip this exercise because its steps are encompassed in Lab Exercise 1.1.3.

■ PART A: CONFIGURING BASIC SETTINGS ON THE SECOND WINDOWS SERVER 2008 COMPUTER

1. Press Ctrl+Alt+Delete on the even-numbered computer assigned to you, and log on as the default administrator of the local computer. Your username will be Administrator. The password will be MSPress#1 or the password that your instructor or lab proctor assigns to you. The Initial Configuration Tasks (ICT) window will be displayed automatically. Expand the ICT window to fill the full screen if necessary.

2. Click Set time zone. The Date and Time window will be displayed.

3. Click Change time zone. The Time zone settings window will be displayed.

4. In the Time zone drop-down box, select the appropriate time zone, and click OK. You will return to the Date and Time window.

5. Click OK to return to the ICT window.

6. Click Enable automatic updating and feedback. Click Enable Windows automatic updating and feedback (recommended).

7. Click Provide computer name and domain. The System Properties window will be displayed.

Question 8	*What is the current name of your computer?*

8. On the Computer Name tab, click Change. The Computer Name/Domain Changes window will appear.

9. In the Computer name text box, enter **W2K8***yy* for your computer name, where *yy* corresponds to the even-numbered computer that your instructor or lab proctor has assigned to you. Click OK. A Computer Name/Domain Changes dialog box will be displayed, informing you that you must restart your computer to apply these changes. Click OK to acknowledge this dialog box.

10. Click Close to close the System Properties window. You will be prompted to restart your computer to apply the name change. Click Restart Now. Your Windows Server 2008 computer will restart.

■ PART B: CONFIGURING A STATIC IP ADDRESS ON THE SECOND WINDOWS SERVER 2008 COMPUTER

1. Press Ctrl+Alt+Delete on the W2K8*yy* server, and log on as the default administrator of the local computer. Your username will be Administrator. The password will be MSPress#1 or the password that your instructor or lab proctor assigns to you. The ICT window will be displayed automatically.

2. Place a checkmark next to Do not show this window at logon. Click Close to close the ICT window. The Server Manager screen will be displayed automatically. Expand the Server Manager window to fit the full screen if necessary.

Question 9	*What is the current name of your computer?*

3. Click View Network Connections. The Network Connections window will be displayed.

4. Right-click your network connection, and select Properties. The network connection's Properties window will be displayed.

5. Click Internet Protocol Version 4 (TCP/IPv4), and select Properties. The Internet Protocol Version 4 (TCP/IPv4) Properties window will be displayed.

6. Select the Use the following IP address radio button. Enter the following IP address information for the even-numbered computer that you recorded at the beginning of this lab.

   IP Address: for example, 192.168.1.102

   Subnet Mask: for example, 255.255.255.0

   Default Gateway: for example, 192.168.1.1

7. Click OK, and then click Close to save your changes. Close the Network Connections window.

8. Log off of the W2K8*yy* server.

Exercise 1.2.4 (optional)	Configuring a Windows Server 2008 Server Core Computer
Overview	Your manager assigned to you the task of preparing an additional Windows Server 2008 computer running Server Core to function as an infrastructure server in one of your branch offices. To begin, you must set up this third Windows Server 2008 computer with basic configuration information and static IP address settings. Because this server is running the Server Core installation option, you must perform most configurations procedures from the command line.
Outcomes	After completing this exercise, you will know how to: ▲ Log on to a Windows Server 2008 Server Core computer ▲ Modify basic settings on a Windows Server 2008 Server Core computer ▲ Configure network settings on a Windows Server 2008 Server Core computer ▲ Enable remote administration exceptions in the Windows Firewall of a Server Core computer
Completion time	20 minutes
Precautions	If you have completed Lab 1.1, you may skip this exercise because its steps are encompassed in Lab Exercise 1.1.4.

■ PART A: CONFIGURING THE SERVER TIME ZONE AND COMPUTER NAME

1. Press Ctrl+Alt+Delete on the third Windows Server 2008 computer assigned to you, and log on as the default administrator of the local computer. Your username will be Administrator. The password will be MSPress#1 or the password that your instructor or lab proctor assigns to you.

Question 10	*What do you see when you log on to a Server Core computer?*

2. Key **timedate.cpl** at the command prompt, and press Enter. The Date and Time window is displayed.

3. Click Change time zone. The Time zone settings window will be displayed.

4. In the Time zone drop-down box, select the appropriate time zone, and click OK. You will return to the Date and Time window. Click OK to return to the command prompt.

5. Key **hostname** at the command prompt, and press Enter.

Question 11	*What is the current name of the computer?*

6. Key **netdom /?** at the command prompt, and press Enter.

Question 12	*What functions can you perform with the netdom command?*

7. At the command prompt, key **netdom renamecomputer %computername% /newname:CORE*xx***, and press Enter.

Question 13	*What warning is displayed on the screen?*

8. Key **y**, and then press Enter.

Question 14	*What message is displayed on the screen?*

9. Key **shutdown /r** at the command prompt, and press Enter. A pop-up window informs you that Windows will shut down in less than a minute. Click Close, and allow the computer to restart.

■ PART B: CONFIGURING A STATIC IP ADDRESS.

1. Press Ctrl+Alt+Delete on CORE*xx*, and log on as the default administrator of the local computer. Your username will be Administrator. The password will be MSPress#1 or the password that your instructor or lab proctor assigns to you.

2. Key **ipconfig /all** at the command prompt, and press Enter. Scroll through the ipconfig output to see all presented information.

Question 15	Is the server receiving its IP configuration via DHCP? How can you tell?

3. Key **netsh** at the command prompt, and then press Enter. Key **?**, and press Enter.

Question 16	What are some of the subcommands are available from the netsh menu?

4. Key **interface**, and then press Enter. Key **?**, and press Enter.

Question 17	What are some of the subcommands that are available from the interface submenu?

5. Key **ipv4**, and then press Enter. Key **?**, and press Enter.

Question 18	What subcommands are available from the ipv4 submenu?

6. Key **set address name="Local Area Connection" source=static address=<IP Address> mask=<Subnet Mask> gateway=<Default Gateway> gwmetric=1**. Press Enter to assign the appropriate static IP configuration as recorded at the beginning of the lab manual. Key **exit** to return to the command prompt.

7. Key **ipconfig /all**, and press Enter.

Question 19	Is the computer's IP address now statically assigned?

8. At the command prompt, key **shutdown /l**, and then press Enter to log off of the CORE*xx* computer.

■ PART C: ENABLING REMOTE ADMINISTRATION OF THE SERVER CORE COMPUTER

1. Press Ctrl+Alt+Delete on the third Windows Server 2008 computer, and log on as the default administrator of the local computer. Your username will be Administrator. The password will be MSPress#1 or the password that your instructor or lab proctor assigns to you.

2. At the command prompt, key **netsh advfirewall set allprofiles settings remotemanagement enable** to allow remote access to the server via the Computer Management MMC, the C$ shares, and so forth, and then press Enter.

3. At the command prompt, key **shutdown /l**, and then press Enter to log off of the computer.

LAB REVIEW QUESTIONS

Completion time   15 minutes

1. In your own words, describe what you learned by completing this lab.

2. Open the Server Manager console on your Windows Server 2008 computer. What selections are available to you in the left pane?

3. Using the Windows Help option, describe any roles and features that are currently installed on this server.

4. Explain in your own words why it is a best practice to configure a server, such as a DNS server, with a static IP address rather than allowing it to obtain an IP address using DHCP.

5. Explore the netsh command menus. Record three commands that you can issue from the command line using netsh, and describe what each command does.

LAB CHALLENGE: CONFIGURING THE WINDOWS FIREWALL

Completion time	15 minutes

Your manager just completed the installation of a new file server that will be used in the lucernepublishing.com domain. You want to configure the Windows Firewall to allow the File & Printer exception on the server.

After completing this exercise, you will know how to:

▲ Configure a Windows Firewall exception on a Windows Server 2008 computer.

Configure the File & Printer Sharing Windows Firewall exception on each Windows Server 2008 computer. Use the Help and Support function from the Start menu to assist you in this procedure. You will use the Windows Firewall Control Panel applet on the W2K8*xx* and/or W2K8*yy* computers and the netsh command-line utility on the CORE*xx* computer.

LAB 2.1
DEPLOYING ACTIVE DIRECTORY

This lab contains the following exercises and activities:

Exercise 2.1.1	Installing Active Directory Domain Services
Exercise 2.1.2	Creating a New Subdomain
Exercise 2.1.3	Administering a Subdomain
Exercise 2.1.4	Removing a Domain
Exercise 2.1.5	Creating a New Forest
Exercise 2.1.6	Administering Forests
Lab Review	Questions
Lab Challenge	Administering Two Forests
Workstation Reset	Returning to Baseline

BEFORE YOU BEGIN

The classroom network consists of Windows Server 2008 student servers that are all connected to a local area network. There is also a classroom server, named ServerDC, that is connected to the same classroom network. ServerDC is also running Windows Server 2008 and is the domain controller for a domain named contoso.com. Throughout the labs in this manual, you will be working with the same student server on which you will install, configure, maintain, and troubleshoot application roles, features, and services.

Your instructor should have supplied you with the information needed to fill in the following table:

Student computer name (Server##)	
Student account name (Student##)	

Working with Lab Worksheets

Each lab in this manual requires that you answer questions, shoot screen shots, or perform other activities that you are to document in a worksheet named for the lab, such as lab01_worksheet. Your instructor will supply you with the worksheet files by copying them to the Students\Worksheets share on ServerDC. As you perform the exercises in each lab, open the appropriate worksheet file using WordPad, fill in the required information, and save the file to your computer's Student##\Documents folder. This folder is automatically redirected to the ServerDC computer. Your instructor will examine these worksheet files to assess your performance.

The procedure for opening and saving a worksheet file is as follows:

1. Click Start, and then click Run. The Run dialog box appears.

2. In the Open text box, key **\\ServerDC\Students\Worksheets\lab##_worksheet** (where lab## contains the number of the lab you're completing), and click OK.

3. The worksheet document opens in Wordpad.

4. Complete all of the exercises in the worksheet.

5. In WordPad, choose Save As from the File menu. The Save As dialog box appears.

6. In the File Name text box, key **lab##_worksheet_*yourname*** (where lab## contains the number of the lab you're completing and *yourname* is your last name), and click Save.

> **NOTE**
> *During sections of this lab, you will be changing your computer's domain affiliation, and the ServerDC computer will not be accessible. During these times, you can save the worksheet file to a local folder and copy it to your Student##\Documents folder at the end of the exercise.*

SCENARIO

You are a newly hired administrator for Contoso, Ltd., assigned to work in the company's testing lab. The company will be introducing a new division in the near future, and you are testing various ways of integrating the division into the company's Active Directory namespace.

After completing this lab, you will be able to:

- Install the Active Directory Domain Services role

- Create a subdomain

- Create a new forest

Estimated lab time: 130 minutes

Exercise 2.1.1	Installing Active Directory Domain Services
Overview	The IT director has decided that the new division should have its own domain, and your first assignment is to build the domain controller for that domain on a Windows Server 2008 computer. In this exercise, you install the Active Directory Domain Services role.
Completion time	5 minutes

1. Turn on your computer. When the logon screen appears, log on to the domain with your Student## account, where ## is the number assigned by your instructor, using the password *P@ssw0rd*.

2. Click Start, point to Administrative Tools, and click Server Manager. Click Continue in the User Account Control message box, and the Server Manager console appears.

3. Select the Roles node, and click Add Roles. The Add Roles Wizard appears, displaying the *Before You Begin* page.

4. Click Next to continue. The *Select Server Roles* page appears.

5. Select the Active Directory Domain Services role, and click Next. The *Active Directory Domain Services* page appears.

6. Click Next to continue. The *Confirm Installation Selections* page appears.

7. Click Install. The wizard installs the role.

8. Click Close. The wizard closes.

9. Close the Server Manager console.

10. Leave the computer logged on for the next exercise.

Exercise 2.1.2	Creating a New Subdomain
Overview	The first domain configuration you have been instructed to test is a subdomain beneath the company's existing contoso.com domain. In this exercise, you create the new subdomain by promoting your server to a domain controller.
Completion time	15 minutes

1. Click Start, and then click Run. The Run dialog box appears.

2. In the Open text box, key **dcpromo.exe**, and click OK. Click Continue in the User Account Control message box. The Active Directory Domain Services Installation Wizard appears, displaying the Welcome page, as shown in Figure 2-1-1.

Figure 2-1-1
Active Directory Domain Services Installation Wizard

3.   Select the Use advanced mode installation checkbox, and click Next. The *Operating System Compatibility* page appears.

4.   Click Next to continue. The *Choose a Deployment Configuration* page appears.

5.   Select the Existing Forest option. Select the Create a new domain in an existing forest option, and then click Next. The *Network Credentials* page appears.

6.   Click Next to accept the default settings. The *Name The New Domain* page appears.

7.   In the Single-label DNS name of the child domain text box, key **domain##**, where ## is the number assigned to your computer.

Question 1	What is the fully qualified domain name (FQDN) of the new domain you are creating?

8.   Click Next. An Active Directory Domain Services Installation Wizard message box appears, warning you that your credentials might not be sufficient to create the new domain.

9.   Click No, and then click Back to return to the *Network Credentials* page.

10. Select the Alternate credentials option, and then click Set. A Windows Security dialog box appears.

11. In the User name text box, key **Administrator**. In the Password text box, key **P@ssw0rd**, and click OK.

12. Click Next. The *Name the New Domain* page appears again with the domain name you specified still in place.

13. Click Next. The *Domain NetBIOS Name* page appears.

14. Click Next to accept the default value. The *Set Domain Functional Level* page appears.

15. In the Domain functional level drop-down list, select Windows Server 2008, and click Next. The *Select a Site* page appears.

16. Click Next to accept the default site name. The *Additional Domain Controller Options* page appears.

Question 2	Why is the Read-only domain controller (RODC) option grayed out on the Additional Domain Controller Options page?

17. Select the Global Catalog checkbox, and click Next. A Static IP Assignment message box appears, warning that the computer has dynamically assigned IP addresses.

18. Click Yes. The *Source Domain Controller* page appears.

19. Click Next to accept the default setting. The *Location for Database, Log Files, and SYSVOL* page appears.

20. Click Next to accept the default settings. The *Directory Services Restore Mode Administrator Password* page appears.

21. In the Password and Confirm Password text boxes, key **P@ssw0rd**, and click Next. The *Summary* page appears.

22. Click Next. The wizard installs Active Directory, and the *Completing the Active Directory Domain Services Installation Wizard* page appears.

23. Click Finish. An Active Directory Domain Services Installation Wizard message box appears, prompting you to restart the computer.

24. Click Restart Now. The computer restarts.

Exercise 2.1.3	Administering a Subdomain
Overview	You have been instructed to configure the new domain so that the administrators of the original contoso.com domain are able to manage it. In this exercise, you use group memberships to provide contoso.com users with access to the new subdomain.
Completion time	20 minutes

1. Log on to the new domain you created with the Domain##\Administrator account, where ## is the number assigned by your instructor, using the password *P@ssw0rd*.

Question 3	*Why can't you log on to the new domain by using your Student## account?*

2. Press Ctrl+Prt Scr to take a screen shot of the Initial Configuration Tasks window, showing the new domain you created in Exercise 2.1.2, and then press Ctrl+V to paste the resulting image into the lab02_1_worksheet file in the page provided.

NOTE	*If the Initial Configuration tasks window does not appear, open the Run dialog box, key **oobe** in the Open text box, and click OK.*

3. Click Start, and then click Administrative Tools > Active Directory Users and Computers. The Active Directory Users and Computers console appears, as shown in Figure 2-1-2.

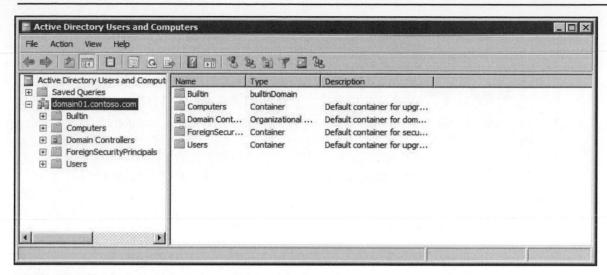

Figure 2-1-2
Active Directory Users and Computers console

4. Right-click the domain##.contoso.com domain and, from the context menu, select New > Organizational Unit. The New Object–Organizational Unit dialog box appears.

5. In the Name text box, key **Sales**, and click OK. The new organizational unit appears in the domain.

6. Right-click the Sales OU that you just created and, from the context menu, select New > User. The New Object–User Wizard appears.

7. In the First name text box, key **Mark**.

8. In the Last name text box, key **Lee**.

9. In the User logon name text box key **mlee** and click Next.

10. In the Password and Confirm password text boxes, key **P@ssw0rd**.

11. Clear the User must change password at next logon checkbox.

12. Select the Password never expires check box, and click Next.

13. Click Finish. The new user object appears in the Sales OU.

14. Right-click the domain##.contoso.com domain and, from the context menu, select Change Domain. The Change Domain dialog box appears.

15. In the Domain text box, key **contoso.com**, and click OK. The contoso.com domain appears in the console.

16. Right-click the contoso.com domain, and examine the context menu.

| **Question 4** | *Why are you unable to create new organizational unit or user objects in the contoso.com domain?* |

17. Open the Change Domain dialog box again, and change back to the domain##.contoso.com domain.

18. Expand the domain##.contoso.com domain, and select the Builtin container.

19. Right-click the Administrators group and, from the context menu, select Properties. The Administrators Properties sheet appears.

20. Click the Members tab, and then click Add. The Select Users, Contacts, Computers, Or Groups dialog box appears.

21. Click Locations. The Locations dialog box appears.

22. Select the contoso.com domain object, and click OK.

23. In the Enter the object names to select box, key **Students**, and click OK. The Students group appears in the Members list.

24. Click OK to close the Administrators Properties sheet.

| **Question 5** | *Are you now able to create new objects in the contoso.com domain? Why or why not?* |

25. Log off of the domain, and log on again by using your contoso.com\Student## account and the password *P@ssw0rd*.

26. Open the Active Directory Users and Computers console, and try to create a new user in the Sales OU by using the name Tracy Tallman and the password *P@ssw0rd*.

| **Question 6** | *Are you now able to create new objects in the domain##.contoso.com domain while logged in with a contoso.com user account? Why or why not?* |

27. Close the Active Directory Users And Groups console.

28. Log off of the computer.

Exercise 2.1.4	Removing a Domain
Overview	In this exercise, you remove the domain you created prior to creating a new forest.
Completion time	10 minutes

1. Log on to the contoso.com domain using the Administrator account and the password *P@ssw0rd*.

2. Open the Run dialog box, and open dcpromo.exe again. The Active Directory Domain Services Installation Wizard appears.

3. Click Next to bypass the Welcome page. An Active Directory Domain Services Installation Wizard message box appears, warning you that the computer is a global catalog server.

4. Click OK. The *Delete the Domain* page appears.

5. Select the Delete the domain because the server is the last domain controller in the domain checkbox, and click Next. The *Application Directory Partitions* page appears.

6. Click Next to continue. The *Confirm Deletion* page appears.

7. Select the Delete all application directory partitions on this Active Directory domain controller checkbox, and click Next. The *Network Credentials* page appears.

8. Click Next to accept the default settings. The *Remove DNS Delegation* page appears.

9. Click Next to accept the default Delete the DNS delegations pointing to this server setting.

10. The *Administrator Password* page appears.

11. In the Password and Confirm Password text boxes, key **P@ssw0rd**, and click Next. The *Summary* page appears.

12. Press Ctrl+Prt Scr to take a screen shot of the *Summary* page, and then press Ctrl+V to paste the resulting image into the lab2_1_worksheet file in the page provided.

13. Click Next to continue. The wizard removes the domain. The *Completing the Active Directory Domain Services Installation Wizard* page appears.

14. Click Finish. An Active Directory Domain Services Installation Wizard message box appears, prompting you to restart the computer.

15. Click Restart Now. The computer restarts.

Exercise 2.1.5	Creating a New Forest
Overview	Another possibility is to create a separate forest for the new division. In this exercise, you promote the domain controller again, this time keeping the new domain completely separate from the existing domain.
Completion time	15 minutes

1. Log on to the local machine as Administrator by using the password *P@ssw0rd*.

Question 7	Now that the domain##.contoso.com domain is gone, why can't you administer the contoso.com domain after logging on with your Student## account?

2. Press Ctrl+Prt Scr to take a screen shot of the Initial Configuration Tasks window, and then press Ctrl+V to paste the resulting image into the lab02_1_worksheet file in the page provided.

3. Open the Run dialog box, and open the dcpromo.exe program once again. The Active Directory Domain Services Installation Wizard appears.

4. Select the Use advanced mode installation checkbox, and click Next. The *Operating System Compatibility* page appears.

5. Click Next to continue. The *Choose a Deployment Configuration* page appears.

6. Select the Create *a new domain in a new forest* option, and then click Next. The *Name the Forest Root Domain* page appears.

7. In the FQDN of the forest root domain text box, key **domain##.com**, where ## is the number assigned to your computer by your instructor, and click Next. The *Domain NetBIOS Name* page appears.

8. Click Next to accept the default NetBIOS name. The *Set Forest Functional Level* page appears.

9. In the Forest functional level drop-down list, select Windows Server 2008, and click Next. The *Additional Domain Controller Options* page appears.

10. Click Next to accept the default settings. A Static IP Assignment message box appears, warning that the computer has dynamically assigned IP addresses.

11. Click Yes. An Active Directory Domain Services Installation Wizard message box appears, warning that the wizard cannot locate an authoritative zone for the domain.

12. Click Yes to continue. The *Location for Database, Log Files, and SYSVOL* page appears.

13. Click Next to accept the default settings. The *Directory Services Restore Mode Administrator Password* page appears.

14. In the Password and Confirm Password text boxes, key **P@ssw0rd**, and click Next. The *Summary* page appears.

15. Click Next. The wizard installs Active Directory, and the *Completing the Active Directory Domain Services Installation Wizard* page appears.

16. Click Finish. An Active Directory Domain Services Installation Wizard message box appears, prompting you to restart the computer.

17. Click Restart Now. The computer restarts.

Exercise 2.1.6	Administering Forests
Overview	In this exercise, you examine the administrative capabilities of the two forests in your Active Directory namespace.
Completion time	15 minutes

1. Log on to domain##.com with the Administrator account by using the password *P@ssw0rd*.

2. Click Start, and then click Administrative Tools > Active Directory Users and Computers. The Active Directory Users and Computers console appears.

3. Expand the domain##.com domain, as shown in Figure 2-1-3.

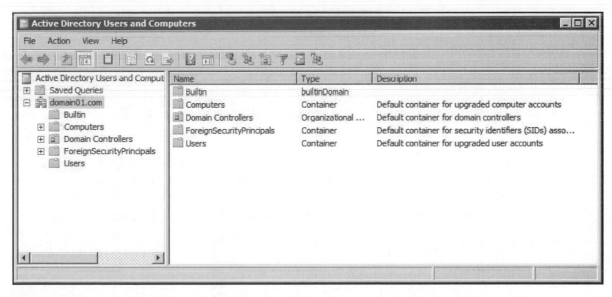

Figure 2-1-3
Domain##.com domain in the Active Directory Users and Computers console

4. In the domain, create a new organizational unit object named Sales and a new user object in the Sales OU with the name Mark Lee, the user logon name mlee, and the password *P@ssw0rd*.

Question 8	What is the result?

5. Right-click the domain##.com domain and, from the context menu, select Change Domain. The Change Domain dialog box appears.

6. In the Domain text box, key **contoso.com**, and click OK. A message box appears, indicating that the domain could not be found.

7. Click OK, and then click Cancel in the Change Domain dialog box.

Question 9	Why were you unable to change to the contoso.com domain?

8. Select the Builtin container.

9. Right-click the Administrators group and, from the context menu, select Properties. The Administrators Properties sheet appears.

10. Click the Members tab, and then click Add. The Select Users, Contacts, Computers, Or Groups dialog box appears.

11. Click Locations. The Locations dialog box appears.

Question 10	Why does the contoso.com domain not appear in the Locations dialog box?

12. Press Ctrl+Prt Scr to take a screen shot of the Locations dialog box, and then press Ctrl+V to paste the resulting image into the lab02_1_worksheet file in the page provided.

13. Click Cancel three times to close the Locations dialog box; the Select Users, Contacts, Computers, or Groups dialog box; and the Administrators Properties sheet.

14. Close the Active Directory Users and Computers console.

15. Log off of the computer.

LAB REVIEW QUESTIONS

Completion time	10 minutes

1. In Exercise 2.1.2, if you selected the Create a new domain tree root checkbox instead of the Create a new child domain checkbox, how would the configuration of the contoso.com forest be different?

2. In Exercise 2.1.2, what was the difference between the Student## account you use to log on at the beginning of the lab and the domain Administrator account that enabled you to successfully create a new subdomain?

3. In Exercise 2.1.2, how many domain trees are in your Active Directory namespace after you create the new domain? How many forests?

4. In Exercise 2.1.5, how many domain trees are in your Active Directory namespace after you create the new domain (not counting the other student computers in the classroom)? How many forests?

LAB CHALLENGE: ADMINISTERING TWO FORESTS

Completion time	20 minutes

In Exercise 2.1.6, you were unable to administer the contoso.com domain while logged on to the new domain##.com forest you created. To complete this challenge, you must configure your computer so that you are able to create Active Directory objects in both domains using a single logon. List the steps you took to achieve this goal. Press Ctrl+Prt Scr to take a screen shot of the Active Directory Users And Computers console, showing the contoso.com domain, and then press Ctrl+V to paste the resulting image into the lab02_1_worksheet file in the page provided.

WORKSTATION RESET: RETURNING TO BASELINE

Completion time	20 minutes

To return the computer to its baseline state, complete the following procedures.

1. Repeat the procedure in Exercise 2.1.4 to remove the domain##.com domain.

2. Restart the computer.

3. Open the Server Manager console, and remove the Active Directory Domain Services and DNS Server roles that you installed during the course of the lab.

4. Restart the computer.

5. In the Initial Configuration Tasks window, click Configure Networking.

6. Right-click the Local Area Connection icon and, from the context menu, select Properties. The Local Area Connection Properties sheet appears.

7. Select the Internet Protocol Version 4 (TCP/IPv4) component, and click Properties. The Internet Protocol Version 4 (TCP/IPv4) Properties sheet appears.

8. Select the Obtain DNS server address automatically option, and click OK.

9. Click OK again to close the Local Area Connection Properties sheet.

10. In the Initial Configuration Tasks window, click Provide Computer Name and Domain. The System Properties sheet appears.

11. Click Change. The Computer Name/Domain Changes dialog box appears.

12. Click More. The DNS Suffix and NetBIOS Computer Name dialog box appears.

13. Clear the Primary DNS Suffix of this Computer text box, and click OK.

14. Select the Domain option. Key **contoso.com** in the text box, and then click Next. The Windows Security dialog box appears.

15. In the User Name text box, key **Student##**.

16. In the Password text box, key **P@ssw0rd**, and click OK. A Computer Name/Domain Changes message box appears, welcoming you to the domain.

17. Click OK twice.

18. Click Close to close the System Properties sheet and restart the computer.

LAB 2.2
CREATING AND MANAGING USERS AND GROUPS

This lab contains the following projects and activities:

BEFORE YOU BEGIN

Lab 2.2 assumes that you have completed the setup process as specified in the setup document and that your computer has connectivity to other lab computers and the Internet. Lab 2.2 also assumes that you have completed the nonoptional exercises in the previous labs. Specifically, Lab 2.2 assumes the following:

- The even-numbered computer (RWDC*yy*) must be configured to use the odd-numbered computer (RWDC*xx*) as its preferred DNS server.
- Active Directory is installed on the odd-numbered computer (RWDC*xx*).
- Active Directory is installed on the even-numbered computer (RWDC*yy*).

> **NOTE**
>
> *In this lab, you will see the characters xx, yy, and zz. These directions assume that students are working in pairs, and that each student has a number. One number is odd and the other number is even. For example, the first student pair will consist of RWDC01 as the first odd-numbered computer and RWDC02 as the first even-numbered computer, RWDC03 and RWDC04 as the second student pair, and RWDC05 and RWDC06 as the third student pair. When you see "xx" in this manual, substitute the unique number assigned to the odd-numbered computer in a pair. When you see "yy", substitute the unique number assigned to the even-numbered computer in a pair.* **When you see "zz", substitute the number assigned to the computer that you are currently working at, regardless of whether it is odd or even.**

SCENARIO

You are the network administrator of Adventure Works. Adventure Works has a multiple-domain Active Directory forest. You manage all network operations. In the near future, you will add network administrators to support your organization. Before you begin to assign responsibilities to these new administrators, you want to be sure that you understand what tasks built-in administrative accounts allow you to perform. You do not want to assign these new administators more rights than necessary to perform their assigned roles.

In addition to assigning roles appropriately, you must develop an administrative hierarchy. You know that the company will have many different administrators, and you do not want to add them directly into the domain local or built-in groups. You want to separate the administrative hierarchy so that you can manage groups of administrators and groups of permissions. During this lab, you will perform several tasks.

After completing this lab, you will be able to:

- Create administrative user accounts.

- Change primary group memberships.

- Identify which built-in administrative groups have the permissions necessary to create sites, create and manager users, view the Active Directory schema, and modify the Active Directory schema.

- Create global and universal groups and use them to assign permissions to user accounts.

- Use dsadd to add users and organizational units (OUs).

- Make changes to user accounts with LDAP Data Interchange Format Directory Exchange (LDIFDE).

Estimated lesson time: 130 minutes

Project 2.2.1	Creating Administrative Accounts
Overview	You are planning to assign new administrators to the built-in groups to create sites and users and to access the Active Directory schema. You must determine which types of built-in groups give the appropriate levels of access. Before you do this, you must create test user accounts for your experiments.
Outcomes	After completing this exercise, you will know how to: • Create a user account.
Completion time	20 minutes
Precautions	Part A and Part C should be performed on the odd-numbered RWDC*xx* computer. Part B should be performed on the even-numbered RWDC*yy* computer. Part D should be performed on both computers.

■ PART A: Creating Administrative Accounts on the Parent Domain

1. Press Ctrl+Alt+Delete on the RWDC*xx* computer and log on as the default domain administrator of the domain*xx* domain. Your username will be Administrator. The password will be MSPress#1 or the password that your instructor or lab proctor has assigned to you. Close the Server Manager screen when it is displayed automatically.

2. To open the Active Directory Users And Computers MMC snap-in, click Start, click Administrative Tools, and then click Active Directory Users And Computers. Expand the domain object domain*xx*.local in the left window pane, if necessary.

3. In the left window pane, right-click the Users container. Click New, and then click User. The New Object–User dialog box is displayed.

4. Create a new user account named DomAdmin in the default Users container. In the Full Name text box, key **DomAdmin**.

5. Click the User Logon Name text box, key **DomAdmin**, the same name used in Step 4, and then click Next.

6. Key **MSPress#1** in the Password text box and in the Confirm Password text box.

7. Clear the User Must Change Password At Next Logon checkbox. Click Next, and then click Finish.

8. Ensure that the Users container is selected. In the right window pane of Active Directory Users And Computers, right-click DomAdmin and click Properties. The DomAdmin Properties dialog box is displayed.

9. Click the MemberOf tab. Click Add. The Select Groups dialog box is displayed.

10. Key **Domain Admins** in the Enter The Object Name To Select text box. Click OK.

11. In the DomAdmin Properties dialog box, click Domain Admins in the MemberOf selection box. Click Set Primary Group to make the primary group Domain Admins.

12. Click Domain Users in the MemberOf selection box. Click Remove to make Domain Admins the only group membership for this user account. A message about removing a user from the group text is displayed. Read the message and click Yes.

13. Click OK in the DomAdmin Properties dialog box.

14. Repeat the previous steps to create two additional accounts named SchAdmin and EntAdmin. Ensure that the SchAdmin account is a member of only the Schema Admins group and that the EntAdmin account is a member of only the Enterprise Admins group.

■ PART B: Creating Administrative Accounts on the Child Domain

1. Press Ctrl+Alt+Delete on the RWDC*yy* computer and log on as the default domain administrator of the child*yy*.domain*xx* domain. Your username will be Administrator. The password will be MSPress#1 or the password that your instructor or lab proctor has assigned to you. Close the Server Manager screen when it is displayed automatically.

2. To open the Active Directory Users And Computers MMC snap-in, click Start, click Administrative Tools, and then click Active Directory Users And Computers. Expand the domain object child*yy*.domain*xx*.local in the left window pane, if necessary.

3. In the left window pane, right-click the Users container. Click New, and then click User. The New Object–User dialog box is displayed.

4. Create a new user account named DomAdmin in the default Users container. In the Full Name text box, key **DomAdmin**.

5. Click the User Logon Name text box, key **DomAdmin**, the same name used in Step 4, and then click Next.

6. Key **MSPress#1** in the Password text box and in the Confirm Password text box.

7. Clear the User Must Change Password At Next Logon checkbox. Click Next, and then click Finish.

8. Verify that the Users container is selected. In the right window pane of Active Directory Users And Computers, right-click DomAdmin and click Properties. The DomAdmin Properties dialog box is displayed.

9. Click the MemberOf tab. Click Add. The Select Groups dialog box is displayed.

10. Key **Domain Admins** in the Enter The Object Name To Select text box. Click OK.

11. In the DomAdmin Properties dialog box, click Domain Admins in the MemberOf selection box. Click Set Primary Group to make the primary group Domain Admins.

12. Select Domain Users in the MemberOf selection box. Click Remove to make Domain Admins the only group membership for this user account. A message about removing a user from the group text is displayed. Read the message and click Yes.

13. Click OK in the DomAdmin Properties dialog box.

14. Repeat the previous steps to create two additional accounts named SchAdmin and EntAdmin. Do not configure group memberships for these accounts, because this will be done in the next part of this project using the odd-numbered computer.

■ PART C: Adding Child User Accounts to Enterprise-wide Administrative Roles

1. Press Ctrl+Alt+Delete on the odd-numbered RWDC*xx* computer and log on as the default domain administrator of the domain*xx* domain. Your username will be Administrator. The password will be MSPress#1 or the password that your instructor or lab proctor has assigned to you. Close the Server Manager screen when it is displayed automatically.

2. To open the Active Directory Users And Computers MMC snap-in, click Start, click Administrative Tools, and then click Active Directory Users And Computers. Expand the domain object domain*xx*.local in the left window pane, if necessary.

3. Verify that the Users container is selected. Right-click the Enterprise Admins group in the right window pane and then click Properties. An Enterprise Admins Properties dialog box is displayed.

4. Click the Members tab and then click Add. The Select Users, Contacts, Computers, Or Groups dialog box is displayed.

5. Click Locations. The Locations dialog box is displayed.

6. Expand the domain*xx*.local object and then expand the child*yy*.domain*xx*.local domain.

7. Click the Users container under the child domain and then click OK.

8. Key **EntAdmin** in the Enter The Object Name To Select text box in the Select Users, Contacts, Computers, Or Groups dialog box. Click Check Names. The EntAdmin user from the child domain should be displayed and underlined. Click OK.

9. Click OK on the Enterprise Admins Properties dialog box.

10. Repeat steps 1 to 9 to add the SchAdmin user account from the child*yy* domain to the Schema Admins group on the parent domain.

■ PART D: Allowing Users to Log On to Domain Controllers

> **NOTE**
>
> *You are about to allow nonadministrative users to log on to a domain controller. You are doing this only for testing purposes; you typically would not want domain users to be able to interactively (locally) log on to a domain controller.*

1. On the odd- and even-numbered computers, open the Group Policy Management Console. Right-click the Default Domain Controllers Policy and click Edit. The Group Policy Management Editor window is displayed.

2. In the left console pane, expand Computer Configuration, expand Policies, expand Windows Settings, expand Security Settings, expand Local Policies, and then click User Rights Assignment.

3. In the right pane, double-click the Allow Logon Locally policy object. The Allow Logon Locally Properties dialog box is displayed.

4. Click Add User Or Group. An Add User Or Group dialog box is displayed.

5. Key **Users** in the User And Group Names text box. Click OK, and then click OK again in the Allow Logon Locally Properties dialog box.

6. Close the Group Policy Management Editor and the Group Policy Management Console.

7. Log off of the odd- and even-numbered computers.

Project 2.2.2   Testing Administrative Access

Overview	You must now test the capabilities of each of the user accounts you created in the previous project.
Outcomes	After completing this exercise, you will know how to: • Test the privileges of Active Directory users.
Completion time	40 minutes
Precautions	Use the DomAdmin, SchAdmin, and EntAdmin administrative accounts created in Project 2.2.1 to complete this activity.

■ PART A: Determine Which Accounts Can Create Sites

1. Log on using the user account being tested, such as DomAdmin. On the odd-numbered RWDC*xx* computer, log onto the domain*xx* domain. On the even-numbered RWDC*yy* computer, log onto the child*yy* domain.

2. Using the Active Directory Sites And Services MMC snap-in, attempt to create a site. Try to create a unique site name with each administrative account. Record the names of the accounts that can be used to create a new site.

Question 1	Which administrative user accounts can create a site?

3. If a site is created successfully, right-click the site name and click Delete in the left window pane of Active Directory Sites And Services. An Active Directory message is displayed. Read the message and click Yes to confirm that you want to delete the site. Another Active Directory message box is displayed. Read the message and click Yes to confirm.

4. Repeat steps 1 through 3 for the SchAdmin and EntAdmin administrative accounts.

■ PART B: Determine Which Accounts Can Create Users

1. Log on using the user account being tested, such as DomAdmin. On the odd-numbered RWDC*xx* computer, log onto the domain*xx* domain. On the even-numbered RWDC*yy* computer, log onto the child*yy* domain.

2. Using the Active Directory Users And Computers MMC snap-in, attempt to create a unique user account on the local domain. Record the names of the accounts that can be used to create new users.

3. Using Active Directory Users And Computers, attempt to create a unique user account on the opposite domain. In the left window pane of the Active Directory Users And Computers console, right-click the Active Directory Users And Computers node and click Connect To Domain. The Connect To Domain dialog box is displayed.

4. Click Browse. The Browse For Domain dialog box is displayed.

5. Select the opposite domain and click OK.

6. In the opposite domain, attempt to create a unique user account. Record the names of the accounts that can be used to create new users.

7. Repeat steps 1 through 6 for the SchAdmin and EntAdmin administrative accounts.

8. Close the Active Directory Users And Computers console and log off.

■ PART C: Determine Which Accounts Can Manage the Schema

1. On the odd-numbered RWDC*xx* computer, log on as the DomAdmin user of the domain*xx* domain. On the even-numbered RWDC*yy* computer, log on as the DomAdmin user of the child*yy* domain.

2. Click the Start button, key **regsvr32 schmmgmt.dll**, and press Enter. Click OK in the message box indicating that the registration succeeded.

3. Click the Start button, key **mmc**, and press Enter. The MMC console is displayed.

4. Click File, and then click Add/Remove Snap-in. The Add/Remove Snap-in window is displayed.

5. Click Add. The Add Standalone Snap-In dialog box is displayed.

6. Locate and click the Active Directory Schema snap-in.

7. Click Add, and then click Close. The Add/Remove Snap-In dialog box is displayed.

8. Click OK.

9. Expand the Active Directory Schema node to reveal the Classes and Attribute nodes.

10. Click Attributes. A list of schema attributes will be displayed in the right window pane.

11. Right-click the Attributes object. If you see that the option to Create Attribute is gray in the context menu, then this user account does not have the ability to modify the schema.

12. Click the File menu, and then click Save As.

13. Key **c:\schema.msc** in the File Name text box. Click Save and close the Schema console.

14. Log off of the local computer.

15. Log on as the SchAdmin user of the local domain.

16. Click Start, key **c:\schema.msc**, and press Enter. The Schema console should be displayed. If you can view the list of Active Directory Schema attributes, the user account has the ability to view the schema. You may need to enter your password again.

17. Right-click the Attributes object. If you see that the Create Attribute option is available in the context menu, the user account has the ability to modify the schema.

18. Log off and log on as the EntAdmin user. Repeat steps 16 through 18 to determine whether the EntAdmin user has the ability to view and/or modify the schema.

Project 2.2.3   Configuring Groups and Permissions

Overview	You must now create an administrative structure that you can use for new administrators. Group administrators into separate global groups. Then, create a universal group that can be used to give new administrators permissions equivalent to the local administrators of each domain.
Outcomes	After completing this exercise, you will know how to: • Create group objects. • Assign permissions to a group.
Completion time	15 minutes
Precautions	N/A

■ PART A: Creating Global Groups

1. On the odd-numbered RWDC*xx* computer, log on as the default administrator of the domain*xx*.local domain.

2. Open the Active Directory Users And Computers console.

3. Expand the domain*xx*.local domain, and then right-click the Users container.

4. Click New, and then click Group. The New Object–Group dialog box is displayed. Notice that the Group Scope default is Global and the Group Type default is Security. Keep these default settings.

5. Key **LAdmins*xx*** in the Group Name text box and click OK.

6. On the even-numbered RWDC*yy* computer, log on as the default administrator of the child*xx* domain.

7. Open the Active Directory Users And Computers console.

8. Expand the child*yy*.domain*xx*.local domain, and then right-click the Users container.

9. Click New, and then click Group. The New Object–Group dialog box is displayed. Notice the Group Scope default is Global and the Group Type default is Security. Keep these default settings.

10. Key **LAdmins*yy*** in the Group Name text box. Click OK.

■ PART B: Creating Universal Groups

1. On the odd-numbered RWDC*xx* computer, right-click the Users container.

2. Click New, and then click Group. The New Object–Group dialog box is displayed.

3. Key **LAdmins** in the Group Name text box.

4. In the Group Scope area, select the Universal radio button. Verify that the Group Type is set to Security and click OK.

5. Verify that the Users container is selected. In the right pane of Active Directory Users And Computers, right-click LAdmins, and then click Properties.

6. Click the Members tab. Click Add. The Select Users, Contacts, Computers, Or Groups dialog box is displayed.

7. Key **LAdmins*xx*** in the Enter The Object Names To Select text box, and then click OK. Remember that LAdmins*xx* is a global group.

8. Click Add again. The Select Users, Contacts, Computers, Or Groups dialog box is displayed again.

9. Click Locations. The Locations dialog box is displayed.

10. Expand the parent domain, and then expand the child domain.

11. Click the Users container under the child domain, and then click OK.

12. Key **LAdmins*yy*** in the Enter The Object Names To Select text box, and then click OK. Remember that LAdmins*yy* is a global group.

13. Click the Member Of tab and click Add. The Select Groups dialog box is displayed.

14. Key **Administrators** in the Enter The Object Names To Select text box. Click OK.

15. Click Add again. The Select Groups dialog box is displayed.

16. Click Locations. The Locations dialog box is displayed.

17. Expand the parent domain.

18. Click the child domain and click OK.

19. Key **Administrators** in the Enter The Object Names To Select text box, and then click OK.

20. Click OK in the LAdmins Properties dialog box.

■ PART C: Assigning Permissions Through Group Membership

1. On the odd-numbered RWDC*xx* computer, create a user acount named LocalAdmin*xx* on the parent domain. Refer to Project 2.2.1, Creating Administrative Accounts on the Parent Domain.

2. Make the LocalAdmin*xx* user a member of the LAdmins*xx* group.

3. On the even-numbered RWDC*yy* computer, create a user account named LocalAdmin*yy* on the child domain. Refer to Project 2.2.1, Creating Administrative Accounts on the Child domain.

4. Make the LocalAdmin*yy* user a member of the LAdmins*yy* group.

5. Log off and log on to each computer with its newly-created user account.

Question 2	*Can you perform administrative tasks, such as creating a user account, shutting down the server, or setting the time, on the domain controllers? Explain the group membership chain that provides this user account with its current permissions.*

6. Log off of both computers.

Project 2.2.4	Using dsadd to Add a User Account
Overview	Your organization is growing and you need to add new OUs and users.
Outcomes	After completing this exercise, you will know how to: • Create an OU from the command line. • Create a user from the command line.
Completion time	10 minutes
Precautions	N/A

■ PART A: Using dsadd to Create an OU and User in the Parent Domain

A Sales department was added to your organizational structure, and you decide to create a new OU to help you manage the resources of this new department. Additionally, a new manager, Kim Ralls, was just hired for the Sales department. You must create a user account for Kelly in the new OU. Use dsadd to add these new objects.

1. On the odd-numbered RWDC*xx* computer, log on as the default administrator of the domain*xx* domain.

2. Open a command-prompt window.

3. Key **dsadd ou ou=Sales,dc=domain*xx*,dc=local –desc Lab2** in the command-prompt window, and then press Enter.

4. Key **dsadd user cn=Kim,ou=Sales,dc=domain*xx*,dc=local –pwd MSPress#1 –samid KimR–upn Kim@domain*xx*.local** in the command-prompt window. Press Enter.

5. Open the Active Directory Users And Computers console and verify that the Sales OU exists and that the Kim user accounts exists inside the OU.

■ PART B: Using dsadd to Create an OU and User in the Child Domain

A Service department was added to your organizational structure, and you decide to create a new OU to help you manage the resources of this new department. Additionally, a new manager, Ajay Solanki, was just hired for the Service department. You must create a user account for Jeff in the new OU. Use dsadd to add these new objects.

1. On the even-numbered RWDC*yy* computer, log on as the default administrator of the child*yy* domain.

2. Open a command-prompt window.

3. Key **dsadd ou ou=Service,dc=child*yy*,dc=domain*xx*,dc=local –desc Lab2** in the command-prompt window. Press Enter.

4. Key **dsadd user cn=Ajay,ou=Service,dc=child*yy*,dc=domain*xx*,dc=local –pwd MSPress#1 –samid AjayS –upn Ajay@child*yy*.domain*xx*.local** in the command-prompt window. Press Enter.

5. Open the Active Directory Users And Computers console and verify that the Service OU exists and that the Ajay user accounts exists inside the OU.

LAB REVIEW QUESTIONS

Completion time	15 minutes

1. In your own words, describe what you learned by completing this lab.

2. Name a task that a member of Schema Admins cannot perform that a member of Enterprise Admins or Domain Admins can perform.

3. What command must you run before you can add the Active Directory Schema console as a snap-in to the Microsoft Management Console?

4. What type of administrative membership allows you to add attributes and object classes to the Active Directory database?

LAB CHALLENGE 2.2.1	USING DSADD TO ADD A USER ACCOUNT TO THE USERS CONTAINER
Overview	Lolan Song and Mike Nash are new employees. Use dsadd to create user accounts for them in the appropriate domain.
Outcomes	After completing this exercise, you will know how to: • Use dsadd to create a user account.
Completion time	10 minutes
Precautions	N/A

Task 1: On the odd-numbered RWDC*xx* computer, use dsadd to create a user account for Lolan Song in the Users container of the domain*xx* domain. Lolan's username should be Lolan, and her pre–Windows 2000 username should by LolanS. Her User Principal Name (UPN) should be lolan@domain*xx*.com. Set her password to MSPress#1.

Task 2: On the even-numbered RWDC*yy* computer, use dsadd to create a user account for Mike Nash in the Users container of the child*yy* domain. Mike's user logon name should be Mike, and his pre–Windows 2000 user logon name should bc MikeN. Set his password to MSPress#1. His UPN should be mike@child*yy*.domain*xx*.local.

LAB CHALLENGE 2.2.2	CHANGING THE UPN SUFFIX WITH LDIFDE
Overview	Lolan and Mike say that they need the UPN suffix contoso.com. They want to be able to log on as Lolan@contoso.com and Mike@contoso.com, respectively.
Outcomes	Use LDIFDE to modify user accounts.
Completion time	20 minutes
Precautions	N/A

Modify the accounts you created for Lolan and Mike using an LDIFDE file to change the UPN. Create one file to be used on the odd-numbered RWDC*xx* computer to modify Lolan's account. Create another file to be used on the even-numbered RWDC*yy* computer to modify Mike's account.

LAB 3.1

CONFIGURING AND MANAGING THE DHCP SERVER ROLE

This lab contains the following exercises and activities:

Exercise 3.1.1   Installing the DHCP Server Role

Exercise 3.1.2   Confirming DHCP Server Functionality

Exercise 3.1.3   Managing the DHCP Server Role

Exercise 3.1.4   Installing and Configuring the DHCP Server Role on Server Core (optional)

Lab Review   Questions

Lab Challenge   Authorizing a DHCP Server in Active Directory

Lab Cleanup

BEFORE YOU BEGIN

Lab 3.1 assumes that setup has been completed as specified in the setup document and that your computer has connectivity to other lab computers and the Internet. The required exercises in Lab 3.1 also assume that you have completed the required exercises in Lab 1.1. Exercise 3.1.4 assumes that you have completed Exercise 1.1.4 in Lab 1.1.

The instructor PC is preconfigured as a domain controller in the lucernepublishing.com domain for demonstration purposes and is named INSTRUCTOR01.

In a multi-student classroom, the instructor should also assign a separate DHCP scope to each student or student pairing so that there are no overlapping DHCP scopes in the room. In a Virtual PC environment, this can also be accomplished by configuring the student VMs on separate virtual networks for the duration of Lab 3.1.

NOTE	*If a DHCP scope is running on the INSTRUCTOR computer or on a hardware-based device such as a classroom router, this must be disabled prior to performing these steps.*

NOTE	*In this lab manual, you will see the characters xx, yy, and zz. These directions assume that you are working on computers configured in pairs and that each computer has a number. One number is odd, and the other number is even. For example, W2K801 is the odd-numbered computer, and W2K802 is the even-numbered computer. When you see xx, substitute the unique number assigned to the odd-numbered computer. When you see yy, substitute the unique number assigned to the even-numbered computer. When you see zz, substitute the number assigned to the computer that you are working at, either odd or even.*

The four Windows Server 2008 server computers referenced in this lab will each be configured with static IP addresses. For ease of reference, record the static IP addresses of each server that you will be working with in this lab:

INSTRUCTOR01 (Instructor Computer)

IP Address: ___.___.___.___

Subnet Mask: ___.___.___.___

Default Gateway: ___.___.___.___

W2K8*xx*: (For example: W2K801)

IP Address: ___.___.___.___

Subnet Mask: ___.___.___.___

Default Gateway: ___.___.___.___

W2K8*yy*: (For example: W2K802)

IP Address: ___.___.___.___

Subnet Mask: ___.___.___.___

Default Gateway: ___.___.___.___

CORE*xx*: (For example: CORE01)

IP Address: ___.___.___.___

Subnet Mask: ___.___.___.___

Default Gateway: ___.___.___.___

SCENARIO

You are a network administrator for Litware, Inc. Recently, Contoso, Ltd. acquired Litware, Inc. As a result, Litware, Inc. is expanding its network. In the past, Litware, Inc. utilized Automatic Private IP Addressing (APIPA). Because of the increase in the number of clients (which motivated Contoso to acquire Litware, Inc.) and the fact that network administrators installed a router to allow users Internet access, you have been asked to plan and install a dynamic addressing system using Dynamic Host Configuration Protocol (DHCP). You and a partner must work together to install the DHCP Server service and configure it to assign the necessary configuration parameters.

After completing this lab, you will be able to:

- Install and configure the DHCP Server role

- Manage the DHCP Server role

- (Optional) Install and configure the DHCP Server role on a Server Core computer

Estimated lab time: 115 minutes

Exercise 3.1.1	Installing the DHCP Server Role
Overview	You have just procured a new server to act as a DHCP server on your network.
Outcomes	After completing this exercise, you will know how to: ▲ Install the DHCP Server role ▲ Configure a DHCP scope
Completion time	20 minutes
Precautions	N/A

1. Press Ctrl+Alt+Delete on the W2K8*xx* Windows Server 2008 computer assigned to you, and log on as the default administrator of the local computer. Your username will be Administrator. The password will be MSPress#1 or the password that your instructor or lab proctor assigns to you.

2. If the Initial Configuration Tasks (ICT) screen window opens automatically, place a checkmark next to Do not show this window at logon, and click Close.

3. If the Server Manager window does not appear automatically, click the Start button, and then click Server Manager.

Question 1	What is the name of the computer you are working from?

4. In the left-hand pane of Server Manager, double-click Roles.

5. Click Add Roles. Click Next to bypass/dismiss the initial Welcome screen.

6. The Select Server Roles screen appears. Place a checkmark next to DHCP Server, and then click Next.

7. The Introduction to DHCP Server screen appears. Click Next.

8. If the Select Network Bindings screen appears, accept the default selection, and click Next. The Specify IPv4 DNS Server Settings screen appears. Leave these settings blank (you will configure them in a later exercise), and click Next

9. The Specify IPv4 WINS Server Settings screen appears. Confirm that the WINS is not required for applications on this network radio button is selected, and click Next.

10. The Add or Edit DHCP Scopes screen appears. Click Add.

11. The Add Scope screen appears. Enter the following information, and click OK.

    - Scope Name: **70-642 Lab 3 Exercise 3-1 Scope**

    - Starting IP Address: The starting IP address that has been assigned by your instructor or lab proctor

    - Ending IP Address: The ending IP address that has been assigned by your instructor or lab proctor

    - Subnet Mask: The subnet mask that has been assigned by your instructor or lab proctor

    - Default Gateway: The default gateway that has been assigned by your instructor or lab proctor

- Subnet Type: Wired

Question 2	*What is the default lease duration of a Wired subnet type?*

12. Click Next. The Configure DHCPv6 Stateless Mode screen appears.

13. Click Next twice, and then click Install. Click Close.

14. You will be returned to the Server Manager console. Under the Roles header in the Roles Summary section, click the DHCP Server hyperlink.

15. The DHCP Server window screen appears. Scroll to the Resources and Support section.

Question 3	*What are three recommendations listed in Server Manager for managing the DHCP Server role?*

16. Log off of the W2K8*xx* computer.

Exercise 3.1.2	Confirming DHCP Server Functionality
Overview	Now that you have installed and configured a DHCP server, you must confirm that DHCP clients on your network are able to receive IP address configuration from the server.
Outcomes	After completing this exercise, you will know how to: ▲ Configure Windows Server 2008 dynamic IP addressing ▲ Confirm DHCP server functionality
Completion time	10 minutes
Precautions	These steps should be performed on the even-numbered W2K8yy computer.

1. Press Ctrl+Alt+Delete on the W2K8*yy* Windows Server 2008 computer assigned to you, and log on as the default administrator of the local computer. Your username will be Administrator. The password will be MSPress#1 or the password that your instructor or lab proctor assigns to you.

2. If the Initial Configuration Tasks (ICT) screen window opens automatically, place a checkmark next to Do not show this window at logon, and click Close.

3. If the Server Manager window does not appear automatically, click the Start button, and then click Server Manager.

Question 4	*What is the name of the computer you are working from?*

4. Click View Network Connections. The Network Connections window is displayed.

5. Right-click your network connection, and select Properties. The network connection's Properties window will be displayed.

6. Click Select Internet Protocol Version 4 (TCP/IPv4), and select click Properties. The Internet Protocol Version 4 (TCP/IPv4) Properties window will be displayed.

Question 5	*What IP addressing settings are currently configured?*

7. Select the Obtain an IP address automatically radio button.

8. Click OK, and then click Close two times to save your changes. Close the Network Connections window.

9. Click Start, key **cmd**, and press Enter.

10. At the command prompt, key **ipconfig /renew**.

11. At the command prompt, key **ipconfig /all**.

Question 6	*Is the computer currently configured for DHCP? How can you tell?*

Question 7	*What is the IP address of the DHCP server from which W2K8yy has obtained its IP address?*

Question 8	*If the answer to #7 was not the IP address of the W2K8xx computer, why might this have happened?*

12. At the command prompt, key **exit**, and press Enter to close the command prompt window.

13. Log off of the W2K8*yy* computer.

Exercise 3.1.3	Managing the DHCP Server Role
Overview	Having configured the basics of a Windows Server 2008 DHCP server, you will now perform management and maintenance tasks on the server prior to deploying it into a production environment. You will verify any changes in functionality using the W2K8*xx* server that is currently configured to obtain its IP address via DHCP.
Outcomes	After completing this exercise, you will know how to: ▲ Configure DHCP options ▲ Configure DHCP reservations ▲ Back up and restore DHCP ▲ View APIPA IP addresses ▲ Deactivate a DHCP scope
Completion time	25 minutes
Precautions	Each part of this exercise will be performed on either the odd-numbered W2K8*xx* computer or the even-numbered W2K8*yy* computer. The exercise instructions will indicate on which computer each part is to be performed.

■ PART A: CONFIGURING DHCP OPTIONS

1. Log on to the W2K8*xx* server. Click Start→Administrative Tools→DHCP. Expand the DHCP console to full screen if necessary.

2. Expand the W2K8*xx* node, followed by IPv4, followed by Scope [[<address>] 70-642 Lab 3 Exercise 3-1 Scope].

Question 9	*What nodes appear underneath the DHCP scope that you created in Exercise 3.1.1?*

3. Right-click Scope Options, and click Configure Options....

4. Place a checkmark next to 006 DNS Servers. In the Server name: text box, enter **w2k8xx**, and click Resolve.

Question 10	*What appears in the IP address text box?*

5. Click Add, and then click OK.

6. Log off of the odd-numbered computer.

■ PART B: CONFIRMING THE ADDITION OF THE DHCP OPTION

1. Log on to the W2K8*yy* computer. Open a command prompt, key **ipconfig /renew**, and press Enter.

2. Key **ipconfig /all**, and press Enter.

Question 11	*What value is configured in the DNS Servers: line?*

3. Record the Physical address of the even-numbered computer for use in the next Part C.

4. Log off of the even-numbered computer.

■ PART C: CONFIGURING A DHCP RESERVATION

1. Log on to the odd numbered computer. Click Start→Administrative Tools→DHCP.

2. Expand the W2K8*xx* node, followed by IPv4, followed by Scope [<address>]70-642 Lab 3 Exercise 3-1 Scope].

3. Click Reservations. Right-click Reservations, and select New Reservation….

4. In the Reservation Name text box, enter **W2K8*yy***.

5. In the IP Address: field, enter an available IP address within the scope that you defined at the start of Lab 3.

6. In the MAC address: field, enter the physical address of the even-numbered computer as indicated in the ipconfig /all output from the even-numbered computer.

7. Click Add, and then Close.

8. Expand the Reservations node. Right-click the reservation you just created, and click Configure Options….

9. Place a checkmark next to 006 DNS Servers. Enter the IP address that you configured for the DHCP reservation you just created.

10. Click Add, and then click OK.

11. Close the DHCP MMC, and log off of the W2K8*xx* computer.

■ PART D: CONFIRMING THE DHCP RESERVATION

1. Log on to the W2K8*yy* computer. Open a command prompt, key **ipconfig /renew**, and press Enter.

2. At the command prompt, key **ipconfig /all**, and press Enter.

Question 12	What value is configured in the DNS Servers: line?

3. Log off of the even-numbered computer.

■ PART E: BACKING UP A DHCP SERVER

1. Log on to the W2K8*xx* computer. Click Start→Administrative Tools→DHCP.

2. Right-click the W2K8*xx* node, and click Backup…. The Browse for Folder screen appears.

Question 13	What is the default location for DHCP server backups?

3. Browse to the C:\ top-level folder. Click Make New Folder. Key **backup**, and press Enter to create the C:\backup folder. Select the C:\backup folder, and then click OK.

4. To simulate a failure of the DHCP server, right-click the scope that you created in Exercise 3.1.1, and click Delete. Click Yes twice to confirm.

5. Log off of the odd-numbered computer.

■ PART F: SIMULATING A DHCP FAILURE ON THE CLIENT

1. Reboot the W2K8*yy* computer to simulate the client booting during a failure of the DHCP server.

2. Open a command prompt window. Key **ipconfig**, and press Enter.

Question 14	*What IP address is configured on the W2K8yy computer?*

3. Log off of the even-numbered computer.

■ PART G: RESTORING THE DHCP DATABASE

1. Log on to the W2K8*xx* computer. Click Start→Administrative Tools→DHCP.

2. Right-click the W2K8*xx* node, and click Restore.... The Browse for Folder screen appears.

3. Select the C:\backup folder, and then click OK. Click Yes when prompted to stop and restart the DHCP server service.

NOTE	*If a red down-arrow appears, click F5 to refresh your view until the red arrow changes to green.*

4. Log off of the odd-numbered computer.

■ PART H: CONFIRMING THE RESTORATION ON THE CLIENT

1. Log on to the W2K8*yy* computer. Open a command prompt.

2. Key **ipconfig /renew**, and then press Enter.

Question 15	*What appears in the IP address text box?*

3. Log off of the even-numbered computer.

■ **PART I: DEACTIVATING THE DHCP SCOPE**

1. Log on to the W2K8*xx* computer. Click Start→Administrative Tools→DHCP.

2. Select the DHCP scope; right-click the scope, and click Deactivate. Click Yes to confirm.

3. Log off of the W2K8xx computer.

Exercise 3.1.4 (optional)	Installing and Configuring the DHCP Server Role on Server Core
Overview	To increase the security of servers deployed in several remote offices, you have prepared servers running the Windows Server 2008 Server Core installation option to provide infrastructure services to these offices. You must now prepare one of these servers to function as a DHCP server.
Outcomes	After completing this exercise, you will know how to: ▲ Install the DHCP Server role on Server Core ▲ Create a DHCP scope on Server Core ▲ Configure DHCP options on Server Core
Completion time	30 minutes
Precautions	This exercise will be performed on the *CORExx* Server Core computer that you installed in Exercise 1.1.4 in Lab 1.1.

■ **PART A: INSTALLING AND CONFIGURING THE DHCP SERVER ROLE ON SERVER CORE**

1. Press Ctrl+Alt+Delete on the CORE*xx* Windows Server 2008 Server Core computer assigned to you, and log on as the default administrator of the local computer. Your username will be Administrator. The password will be MSPress#1 or the password that your instructor or lab proctor assigns to you.

2. From the command prompt window, key **start /w ocsetup DHCPServerCore**, and then press Enter.

3. At the command prompt, key **sc config dhcpserver start= auto**, and press Enter.

> **NOTE** *Be sure to include the space between "'=" and "auto" or else the command will fail.*

4. At the command prompt, key **net start dhcpserver**, and press Enter.

5. At the command prompt, key **netsh**, and press Enter. Key **dhcp server**, and press Enter.

6. To create the scope, key **add scope <Scope Address> <Scope Subnet Mask> ServerCoreScope**, and press Enter. For example, key **add scope 192.168.100.0 255.255.255.0 ServerCoreScope**, and press Enter.

7. Key **exit**, and then press Enter.

8. At the command prompt, key **Shutdown /l**, and then press Enter to log off of the CORE*xx* computer.

■ PART B: CONFIRMING DHCP FUNCTIONALITY

1. Log on to the W2K8*yy* computer. Open a command prompt, key **ipconfig /renew**, and then press Enter.

> **NOTE** *If you receive an error message, wait a few minutes and try again.*

2. Key **ipconfig /all**, and then press Enter.

> **Question 16** *From which DHCP server are you receiving an IP address?*

LAB REVIEW QUESTIONS

Completion time	15 minutes

1. In your own words, describe what you learned by completing this lab.

2. You have installed the DHCP Server service on a computer running Windows Server 2008. You configure and activate a 10.0.0.0/24 scope; however, clients still are receiving a 169.254.*x.x* IP address. What should you do?

3. You have configured a DHCP scope with an address range of 192.168.0.1 through 192.168.0.254. You have several servers and printers that use the IP address range of 192.168.0.1 through 192.168.0.20. With the least amount of administrative effort, how can you prevent duplicate IP addressing?

4. You currently are using a DHCP server on your network. It assigns a default gateway scope option to clients. You use a router with a different IP address to replace a router on your network. The new router allows clients to connect to the Internet; however, clients cannot connect to the Internet using the new router. What should you do?

LAB CHALLENGE: AUTHORIZING A DHCP SERVER IN ACTIVE DIRECTORY

Completion time	15 minutes

You have completed the installation of the DHCP Server role on multiple Windows Server 2008 computers. To test DHCP's interoperability with Active Directory, you wish to join one of the DHCP servers to the lucernepublishing.com Active Directory domain that is hosted on the INSTRUCTOR01 Windows Server 2008 computer and then authorize the DHCP server within Active Directory.

After completing this exercise, you will know how to:

▲ Join an Active Directory domain

▲ Authorize a DHCP server in Active Directory

Precautions: If you do not complete the Lab Challenge exercise, you must still complete the Post-Lab Cleanup steps prior to continuing on to Lab 4.1.

Join each computer in this lab to the lucernepublishing.com Active Directory domain that is hosted on the INSTRUCTOR01 Windows Server 2008 computer; use LP\Administrator as the domain credentials to join each computer to the domain with a password of MSPress#1, or else use the credentials provided by your instructor or lab proctor.

> **NOTE** *You will need to configure DNS on each computer to point to INSTRUCTOR01 as its preferred DNS server.*

Once the DHCP server has joined the Active Directory domain, use the DHCP MMC snap-in to authorize the DHCP server within Active Directory. Check the Event Viewer on the DHCP server to confirm that the server has been successfully authorized.

LAB CLEANUP

Completion time   15 minutes

You have completed testing of the DHCP server role, and now need to reset your Windows Server 2008 computers to their original state prior to performing testing of additional infrastructure services that you are planning to deploy to your production network.

After completing this exercise, you will know how to:

▲ Remove the DHCP Server role

PART A: REMOVING THE DHCP SERVER ROLE FROM W2K8*XX*

1. Log on to the W2K8*xx* server. If the Server Manager console does not appear automatically, click the Start button, and then click Server Manager.

2. In the left-hand pane of Server Manager, click Roles. In the right-hand pane, click Remove Roles. Click Next

3. The Remove Server Roles screen appears. Remove the checkmark next to DHCP Server, and then click Next.

4. Click Remove, and then click Close when the removal has completed.

5. When prompted, reboot the W2K8*xx* computer.

6. Log on to the W2K8*xx* server after it reboots. The Server Manager console will reappear automatically. Click Finish when prompted.

7. Log off of the W2K8*xx* server.

PART B: CONFIGURING W2K8*YY* WITH A STATIC IP ADDRESS

Using the IP addresses recorded at the beginning of this lab as a reference, reconfigure the even-numbered W2K8*yy* server with a static IP address, subnet mask, and default gateway.

PART C: REMOVING THE DHCP SERVER ROLE FROM CORE*XX*

1. Log on to the CORE*xx* server. At the command prompt, key **start /w ocsetup DHCPServerCore /uninstall**, and press Enter.

2. When prompted, click Yes to restart the server.

PART D: LAB CHALLENGE CLEANUP

If you completed Lab Challenge 3.1.1, perform the following cleanup tasks:

- Reverse any changes that you made to the IP configuration of any lab computers, including the preferred or alternate IP address settings.

- Any lab computers that you added into the lucernepublishing.com domain should be switched to a workgroup configuration.

LAB 4.1
CONFIGURING AND MANAGING THE DNS SERVER ROLE

This lab contains the following exercises and activities:

Exercise 4.1.1   Installing the DNS Server Role

Exercise 4.1.2   Configuring a Secondary Zone and Zone Transfers

Exercise 4.1.3   Configuring Reverse Lookup Zones and Confirming DNS Functionality

Exercise 4.1.4   Installing and Configuring the DNS Server Role on Server Core (optional)

Lab Review   Questions

Lab Challenge   Configuring DNS Forwarders

Lab Cleanup

BEFORE YOU BEGIN

Lab 4.1 assumes that setup has been completed as specified in the setup document and that your computer has connectivity to other lab computers and the Internet. The required exercises in Lab 4.1 also assume that you have completed the exercises in Lab 1.1. Exercise 4.1.5 assumes that you have completed Exercise 1.1.4 in Lab 1.1.

The instructor PC is preconfigured as a domain controller in the lucernepublishing.com domain for demonstration purposes and is named INSTRUCTOR01.

NOTE

In this lab manual, you will see the characters xx, yy, and zz. These directions assume that you are working on computers configured in pairs and that each computer has a number. One number is odd, and the other number is even. For example, W2K801 is the odd-numbered computer, and W2K802 is the even-numbered computer. When you see xx, substitute the unique number assigned to the odd-numbered computer. When you see yy, substitute the unique number assigned to the even-numbered computer. When you see zz, substitute the number assigned to the computer that you are working at, either odd or even.

The four Windows Server 2008 server computers referenced in this lab will each be configured with static IP addresses. For ease of reference, record the static IP addresses of each server that you will be working with in this lab:

INSTRUCTOR01 (Instructor Computer)

IP Address: ___.___.___.___

Subnet Mask: ___.___.___.___

Default Gateway: ___.___.___.___

W2K8*xx*: (For example: W2K801)

IP Address: ___.___.___.___

Subnet Mask: ___.___.___.___

Default Gateway: ___.___.___.___

W2K8*yy*: (For example: W2K802)

IP Address: ___.___.___.___

Subnet Mask: ___.___.___.___

Default Gateway: ___.___.___.___

CORE*xx*: (For example: CORE01)

IP Address: ___.___.___.___

Subnet Mask: ___.___.___.___

Default Gateway: ___.___.___.___

You will also need two test IP addresses in the same IP subnet for use in a later exercise. Record these IP addresses here for reference:

TEST*xx*: (For example: TEST01)

IP Address: ___.___.___.___

TEST*yy*: (For example: TEST02)

IP Address: ___.___.___.___

SCENARIO

You are a network administrator for Contoso, Ltd. Recently, Lucerne Publishing has entered into a joint venture with another company, Adatum. As a result, both organizations now have a requirement to be able to resolve the names of servers hosting resources in each organization. You have been asked to plan and install the Domain Name System (DNS) service to provide name resolution for users in both networks. You will need to install the DNS Server service and configure it to assign the necessary configuration parameters.

After completing this lab, you will be able to:

- Install the DNS Server Role

- Configure a secondary zone and zone transfers

- Configure reverse lookup zones and confirming DNS functionality

- (Optional) Install and configureg the DNS Server Role on Server Core

Estimated lab time:145 minutes

Exercise 4.1.1	Installing the DNS Server Role
Overview	You have just procured a new server to act as a DNS server on your network.
Outcomes	After completing this exercise, you will know how to: ▲ Install the DNS Server role on Windows Server 2008 ▲ Create primary DNS zones ▲ Create DNS host (A) records
Completion time	20 minutes
Precautions	This exercise will be performed on both the odd-numbered W2K8*xx* computer and the even-numbered W2K8*yy* computer.

■ PART A: INSTALLING THE DNS SERVER ROLE ON THE ODD-NUMBERED COMPUTER

1. Press Ctrl+Alt+Delete on the W2K8*xx* Windows Server 2008 computer assigned to you, and log on as the default administrator of the local computer. Your username will be Administrator. The password will be MSPress#1 or the password that your instructor or lab proctor assigns to you.

2. If the Initial Configuration Tasks (ICT) screen window opens automatically, place a checkmark next to Do not show this window at logon, and click Close.

3. If the Server Manager window does not appear automatically, click the Start button, and then click Server Manager.

Question 1	*What is the name of the computer from which you are working?*

4. In the left-hand pane of Server Manager, double-click Roles.

5. Click Add Roles. Click Next to dismiss the initial Welcome screen.

6. The Select Server Roles screen appears. Place a checkmark next to DNS Server, and then click Next.

7. The Introduction to DNS Server screen appears. Click Next, and then click Install.

8. Click Close when the installation completes.

9. Log off of the odd-numbered computer.

■ PART B: INSTALLING THE DNS SERVER ROLE ON THE EVEN-NUMBERED COMPUTER

1. Press Ctrl+Alt+Delete on the W2K8*yy* Windows Server 2008 computer assigned to you, and log on as the default administrator of the local computer. Your username will be Administrator. The password will be MSPress#1 or the password that your instructor or lab proctor assigns to you.

2. If the ICT screen window opens automatically, place a checkmark next to Do not show this window at logon, and click Close.

3. If the Server Manager window does not appear automatically, click the Start button, and then click Server Manager.

> **Question 2**
>
> *What is the name of the computer from which you are working?*

4. In the left-hand pane of Server Manager, double-click Roles.

5. Click Add Roles. Click Next to dismiss the initial Welcome screen.

6. The Select Server Roles screen appears. Place a checkmark next to DNS Server, and then click Next.

7. The Introduction to DNS Server screen appears. Click Next, and then click Install.

8. Click Close when the installation completes.

9. Log off of the even-numbered computer.

■ PART C: CONFIGURING A PRIMARY ZONE FOR CONTOSO.COM ON THE ODD-NUMBERRED COMPUTER

> **NOTE**
>
> *Be sure to complete these steps on the odd-numbered W2K8xx computer only!*

1. Log on to the odd-numbered W2K8*xx* computer. Click Start→Administrative Tools→DNS. Expand the DNS MMC to full screen if necessary.

2. Navigate to W2K8*xx*→Forward Lookup Zones.

> **Question 3**
>
> *What forward lookup zones are currently configured on the W2K8xx computer?*

3. Right-click Forward Lookup Zones, and click New Zone…. Click Next. The Zone Type screen appears.

Question 4	*What types of zones can you configure from this screen?*

4. Ensure that the Primary zone radio button is selected, and then click Next.

5. The Zone Name screen appears. In the Zone name: text box, key **contoso.com**. Click Next.

6. The Zone File screen appears. Accept the default selection, and click Next.

Question 5	*What is the default selection on the Zone File screen?*

7. The Dynamic Update screen appears. Accept the default selection of "Do not allow dynamic updates," and click Next.

Question 6	*Why is the "allow only secure dynamic updates" option greyed out?*

8. Click Finish. Confirm that contoso.com appears in the list of Forward Lookup Zones configured on W2K8*xx*.

9. Select the contoso.com forward lookup zone.

Question 7	*What records are configured for the contoso.com zone?*

10. Right-click contoso.com, and click New Host (A or AAAA)….

11. The New Host screen appears. In the Name (uses parent domain name if blank): text box, enter **W2K8*xx***. In the IP address: text box, enter the IP address of the W2K8*xx* server.

12. Click Add Host. Click OK, and then click Done to confirm. Confirm that an A record has been added for W2K8*xx*.

13. If the Server Manager console is not open already, click Start→Server Manager. Click View Network Connections.

14. Right-click Local Area Connection, and click Properties. Double-click Internet Protocol Version 4 (TCP/IPv4). In the Use the following DNS server addresses: section, enter the IP address of W2K8*xx* as the preferred DNS server.

15. Click OK twice, and then close the Network Connections window.

16. Log off of the odd-numbered computer.

■ PART D: CONFIGURING A PRIMARY ZONE FOR ADATUM.COM ON THE EVEN-NUMBERED COMPUTER

NOTE	Be sure to complete these steps on the even-numbered W2K8*xxyy* computer only!

1. Log on to the even-numbered W2K8*yy* computer. Click Start→Administrative Tools→DNS. Expand the DNS MMC to full screen if necessary.

2. Navigate to W2K8*yy*→Forward Lookup Zones.

3. Right-click Forward Lookup Zones, and click New Zone…. Click Next. The Zone Type screen appears.

4. Ensure that the Primary zone radio button is selected, and then click Next.

5. The Zone Name screen appears. In the Zone name: text box, key **adatum.com**. Click Next.

6. The Zone File screen appears. Accept the default selection, and click Next.

Question 8	What is the default selection on the Zone File screen?

7. The Dynamic Update screen appears. Accept the default selection of "Do not allow dynamic updates," and click Next.

8. Click Finish. Confirm that adatum.com appears in the list of Forward Lookup Zones configured on W2K8*yy*.

9. Select the adatum.com forward lookup zone.

10. Right-click adatumcontoso.com, and click New Host (A or AAAA)….

11. The New Host screen appears. In the Name (uses parent domain name if blank): text box, enter **W2K8***yy*. In the IP address: text box, enter the IP address of the W2K8*xx* server.

12. Click Add Host. Click OK, and then click Done to confirm. Confirm that an A record has been added for W2K8*yy*.

13. If the Server Manager console is not open already, click Start→Server Manager. View Network Connections.

14. Right-click Local Area Connection, and click Properties. Double-click Internet Protocol Version 4 (TCP/IPv4). In the Use the following DNS server addresses: section, enter the IP address of W2K8*yy* as the preferred DNS server.

15. Click OK twice, and then close the Network Connections window.

16. Log off of the even-numbered computer.

Exercise 4.1.2	Configuring a Secondary Zone and Zone Transfers
Overview	You have configured a server to host a primary DNS zone for the contoso.com and adatum.com DNS domains. You must now configure these servers so that clients in each domain can resolve a fully qualified domain name (FQDN) in their own domain as well as FQDNs in the remote domain.
Outcomes	After completing this exercise, you will know how to: ▲ Create secondary DNS zones ▲ Configure DNS zone transfers
Completion time	25 minutes
Precautions	This exercise will be performed on both the odd-numbered W2K8*xx* computer and the even-numbered W2K8*yy* computer.

■ **PART A: CONFIGURING THE ODD-NUMBERED DNS SERVER TO ALLOW ZONE TRANSFERS TO THE EVEN-NUMBERED DNS SERVER**

1. Log on to the W2K8*xx* computer. Click the Start button, then click Administrative Tools, and then click DNS.

2. Select the W2K8*xx* node, and then expand the Forward Lookup Zones node. Select the contoso.com node. Right-click on the contoso.com node, and select Properties.

3. On the Zone Transfers tab, place a checkmark next to Allow zone transfers.

4. Select the Only to the following servers radio button, and then click Edit.

5. In the IP addresses of the secondary servers section, key the IP address of W2K8*yy*. Press Enter, and click OK. If you plan to complete the optional Server Core exercise, key the IP address of CORE*xx*. Press Enter, and click OK.

6. Log off of the W2K8*xx* computer.

■ PART B: CONFIGURING THE EVEN-NUMBERED DNS SERVER TO ALLOW ZONE TRANSFERS TO THE ODD-NUMBERED DNS SERVER.

1. Log on to the W2K8*yy* computer. Click the Start button, then click Administrative Tools, and then click DNS.

2. Select the W2K8*yy* node, and then expand the Forward Lookup Zones node. Select the contoso.com node. Right-click on the contoso.com node, and select Properties.

3. On the Zone Transfers tab, place a checkmark next to Allow zone transfers.

4. Select the Only to the following servers radio button, and then click Edit.

5. In the IP addresses of the secondary servers section, key the IP address for the W2K8*xx* server, and press Enter. (If you plan to complete the optional Server Core exercise, also key the IP address of the CORE*xx* server, and press Enter.), Click OK twice.

6. Log off of the W2K8*yy* computer.

■ PART C: CONFIGURING A SECONDARY ZONE FOR ADATUM.COM ON THE ODD-NUMBERED SERVER

1. Log on to the odd-numbered W2K8*xx* computer. Click Start→Administrative Tools→DNS. Expand the DNS MMC to full screen if necessary.

2. Expand the Forward Lookup Zones node.

Question 9	What forward lookup zones are currently configured on the W2K8xx computer?

3. Right-click the Forward Lookup Zones node, and select New Zone…. Click Next to dismiss the initial Welcome screen.

4.   On the Zone Type screen, select Secondary Zone, and click Next.

5.   The Zone Name zone screen appears. Enter **adatum.com**. Click Next.

6.   The Master DNS Servers screen appears. Enter the IP address of the W2K8*yy* server, and press Enter. Confirm that it shows a green checkmark next to the IP address and a value of "OK" in the Validated column. Click Next, and then Finish.

7.   Expand the zone for adatum.com, and confirm that you can see an A record for W2K8*yy*.

NOTE	*If you receive an error when you open the secondary zone, wait a few minutes and press F5.*

8.   Log off of the odd-numbered W2K8*xx* computer.

■ PART D: CONFIGURING A SECONDARY ZONE FOR ADATUM.COM ON THE EVEN-NUMBERED SERVER

1.   Log on to the odd-numbered W2K8*yy* computer. Click Start→Administrative Tools→DNS. Expand the DNS MMC to full screen if necessary.

2.   Expand the Forward Lookup Zones node.

Question 10	*What forward lookup zones are currently configured on the W2K8xx computer?*

3.   Right-click the Forward Lookup Zones node, and select New Zone…. Click Next to dismiss the initial Welcome screen.

4.   On the Zone Type screen, select Secondary Zone, and click Next.

5.   The Zone Name zone screen appears. Enter **contoso.com**. Click Next.

6.   The Master DNS Servers screen appears. Enter the IP address of the W2K8*xx* server, and press Enter. Confirm that it shows a green checkmark next to the IP address and a value of "OK" in the Validated column. Click Next, and then Finish.

7. Expand the zone for contoso.com, and confirm that you can see an A record for W2K8*xx*.

> | NOTE | *If you receive an error when you open the secondary zone, wait a few minutes and press F5.* |
> |------|------|

8. Log off of the even-numbered W2K8*yy* computer.

Exercise 4.1.3	Configuring Reverse Lookup Zones and Confirming DNS Functionality
Overview	You have configured a server to host primary and secondary DNS zones for the contoso.com and adatum.com DNS domains. You must now confirm that DNS is functioning correctly on each server. To use troubleshooting tools such as nslookup, you will also need to configure a reverse lookup zone for each DNS server.
Outcomes	After completing this exercise, you will know how to: ▲ Create reverse lookup zones ▲ Testing DNS name resolution (nslookup)
Completion time	25 minutes
Precautions	This exercise will be performed on both the odd-numbered W2K8*xx* computer and the even-numbered W2K8*yy* computer.

■ PART A: CONFIGURING A REVERSE LOOKUP ZONE ON THE ODD-NUMBERED W2K8*XX* COMPUTER

1. Log on to the W2K8*xx* computer. Click the Start button, followed by Administrative Tools, followed by DNS.

2. Click the W2K8*xx* zone, and then click the Reverse Lookup Zones node.

> | Question 11 | *What reverse lookup zones are currently configured on the W2K8xx computer?* |
> |-------------|------|

3. To create a reverse lookup zone, right-click Reverse Lookup Zones in the left-hand pane, and click New Zone….

4. The New Zone Wizard appears. Click Next to dismiss the initial Welcome screen.

5. The Zone Type screen appears. Click Primary zone, and click Next.

6. The Reverse Lookup Zone Name screen appears. Select IPv4 Reverse Lookup Zone, and click Next.

7. Enter the Network ID of your lab network; this value will be 192.168.1 or the value provided by your instructor or lab proctor. Click Next.

8. The Zone File screen appears. Accept the default value, and click Next.

9. The Dynamic Update screen appears. Accept the default selection of "Do not allow dynamic updates," and click Next.

10. Click Finish. Confirm that the Reverse Lookup Zone appears in the DNS management console.

11. Log off of the W2K8*xx* computer.

■ PART B: CONFIGURING A REVERSE LOOKUP ZONE ON THE EVEN-NUMBERED W2K8*YY* COMPUTER

1. Log on to the W2K8*yy* computer. Click the Start button, followed by Administrative Tools, followed by DNS.

2. Click the W2K8*yy* zone, and then click the Reverse Lookup Zones node.

Question 12	What reverse lookup zones are currently configured on the W2K8yy computer?

3. To create a reverse lookup zone, right-click Reverse Lookup Zones in the left-hand pane, and click New Zone....

4. The New Zone Wizard appears. Click Next to bypass the initial Welcome screen.

5. The Zone Type screen appears. Click Primary zone, and click Next.

6. The Reverse Lookup Zone Name screen appears. Select IPv4 Reverse Lookup Zone, and click Next.

7. Enter the Network ID of your lab network; this value will be 192.168.1 or the value provided by your instructor or lab provider. Click Next.

8. The Zone File screen appears. Accept the default value, and click Next.

9. The Dynamic Update screen appears. Accept the default selection of "Do not allow dynamic updates," and click Next.

10. Click Finish. Confirm that the Reverse Lookup Zone appears in the DNS management console.

11. Log off of the W2K8*yy* computer.

■ PART C: SIMULATING A DATA CHANGE AND PERFORMING A ZONE TRANSFER FOR THE CONTOSO.COM ZONE

1. Log on to the W2K8*xx* computer. Click the Start button, then click Administrative Tools, and then click DNS.

2. Expand the W2K8*xx* node, and then expand the Forward Lookup Zones node.

3. Click the contoso.com node, then right-click and select New Host (A or AAAA)....

4. The New Host screen appears. In the Name (uses parent domain name if blank): text box, enter **test*xx***. In the IP address: text box, enter the IP address assigned to you for test*xx*.

5. Click Add Host. Click OK, and then click Done to confirm. Confirm that an A record has been added for test*xx*.

6. Log off of the W2K8xx computer.

7. Log on to the W2K8*yy* computer. Click the Start button, then click Administrative Tools, and then click DNS.

8. Expand the W2K8*yy* node, and then expand the Forward Lookup Zones node.

9. Right-click the contoso.com node, then right-click and select Transfer from Master.

Question 13	What happens to the green "Refresh" button in the DNS MMC when you click "Transfer From Master?"

10. Wait a few minutes, and then press F5 to refresh your view of the contoso.com zone. Confirm that the test*xx* record appears.

11. Log off of the even-numbered computer.

■ PART D: SIMULATING A DATA CHANGE AND PERFORMING A ZONE TRANSFER FOR THE ADATUM.COM ZONE

1. Log on to the W2K8*yy* computer. Click the Start button, then click Administrative Tools, and then click DNS.

2. Expand the W2K8*yy* node, and then expand the Forward Lookup Zones node.

3. Click the adatum.com zone, then right-click and select New Host (A or AAAA)....

4. The New Host screen appears. In the Name (uses parent domain name if blank): text box, enter **testyy**. In the IP address: text box, enter the IP address assigned to you for test*yy*.

5. Click Add Host. Click OK, and then click Done to confirm. Confirm that an A record has been added for test*yy*.

6. Log off of the W2K8*yy* computer.

7. Log on to the W2K8*xx* computer. Click the Start button, then click Administrative Tools, and then click NS.

8. Expand the W2K8*xx* node, and then expand the Forward Lookup Zones node.

9. Click the adatum.com node, then right-click and select Transfer from Master.

10. Wait a few minutes, and then click press F5 to refresh your view of the contoso.com zone. Confirm that the test*yy* record appears.

11. Log off of the odd-numbered computer.

■ PART E: CONFIRMING DNS FUNCTIONALITY ON THE ODD-NUMBERED COMPUTER

1. Log on to the odd-numbered W2K8*xx* computer. Open a command-prompt window.

2. At the command prompt, key **nslookup w2k8yy.adatum.com**, and press Enter. Confirm that the nslookup output matches the A record.

3. At the command prompt, key **nslookup testyy.adatum.com**, and press Enter. Confirm that the nslookup output matches the A record that you created in Part D.

4. Log off of the odd-numbered W2K8*xx* computer.

■ PART F: CONFIRMING DNS FUNCTIONALITY ON THE EVEN-NUMBERED COMPUTER

1. Log on to the even-numbered W2K8*yy* computer. Open a command-prompt window.

2. At the command prompt, key **nslookup w2k8*xx*.contoso.com**, and press Enter. Confirm that the nslookup output is correct.

3. At the command prompt, key **nslookup test*xx*.contoso.com**, and press Enter. Confirm that the nslookup output is correct.

4. Log off of the even-numbered W2K8*yy* computer.

Exercise 4.1.4 (optional)	Installing and Configuring the DNS Server Role on Server Core
Overview	To increase the security of servers deployed in several remote offices, you have prepared servers running the Windows Server 2008 Server Core installation option to provide infrastructure services to these offices. You must now prepare one of these servers to function as a DNS server.
Outcomes	After completing this exercise, you will know how to: ▲ Install the DNS Server role on Windows Server 2008 Server Core ▲ Create secondary DNS zones from the command line ▲ Create DNS host (A) records from the command line
Completion time	30 minutes
Precautions	N/A

■ PART A: INSTALLING AND CONFIGURING THE DNS SERVER ROLE ON SERVER CORE

1. Press Ctrl+Alt+Delete on the CORE*xx* Windows Server 2008 Server Core computer assigned to you, and log on as the default administrator of the local computer. Your username will be Administrator. The password will be MSPress#1 or the password that your instructor or lab proctor assigns to you.

2. From the command prompt window, key **start /w ocsetup DNS-Server-Core-Role,** and then press Enter.

3. Key **sc config dns start= auto**, and press Enter.

> **NOTE** *Be sure to include the space between "'=" and "auto" or else the command will fail.*

4. Key net **start dns**, and press Enter.

> **NOTE** *If you receive an error message that the service has already been started, continue to the next step.*

5. To configure the Server Core computer to point to itself for name resolution, key **netsh int ipv4 add dnsserver "Local Area Connection" <IP Address of CORExx>**, and then press Enter.

■ PART B: CONFIGURING A SECONDARY ZONE FOR CONTOSO.COM AND ADATUM.COM AND FORCING A ZONE TRANSFER

1. At the command prompt, key **dnscmd /zoneadd contoso.com /secondary <IP Address of W2K8xx>,** and press Enter.

2. At the command prompt, key **dnscmd /zonerefresh contoso.com**, and press Enter.

3. At the command prompt, key **dnscmd /zoneadd adatum.com /secondary <IP Address of W2K8yy>**, and press Enter.

4. At the command prompt, key **dnscmd /zonerefresh adatum.com**, and press Enter.

■ PART C: CONFIGURING A REVERSE LOOKUP ZONE

1. At the command prompt, key **dnscmd /zoneadd <Network ID>.in-addr. /primary**.

2. Press Enter.

■ PART D: CONFIRMING DNS FUNCTIONALITY

1. At the command prompt, key n**slookup w2k8xx.contoso.com**, and press Enter. Confirm that the nslookup output is correct.

2. At the command prompt, key **nslookup test***xx***.contoso.com**, and press Enter. Confirm that the nslookup output is correct.

3. At the command prompt, key **nslookup w2k8***yy***.adatum.com**, and press Enter. Confirm that the nslookup output is correct.

4. At the command prompt, key **nslookup test***yy***.adatum.com**, and press Enter. Confirm that the nslookup output is correct.

5. Log off of the CORE*xx* computer.

LAB REVIEW QUESTIONS

Completion time	15 minutes

1. In your own words, describe what you learned by completing this lab.

2. You are able to resolve the names of the W2K8*xx*, W2K8*yy*, and CORE*xx* computers. Are you able to ping these computers? Why or why not?

3. You want to have only secure dynamic updates for a DNS zone file. Which type of zone file must you have?

4. When do you use forwarding with DNS? Give one example.

5. What is the difference between forwarding and conditional forwarding?

LAB CHALLENGE: CONFIGURING DNS FORWARDERS

Completion time	15 minutes

You have completed testing the DNS server service role on multiple Windows Server 2008 computers using primary and secondary zones. You wish to test the use of DNS forwarders because these will need to be used in several remote offices that rely on a local ISP to perform Internet DNS queries.

After completing this exercise, you will know how to:

▲ Delete a DNS zone

▲ Configure a DNS forwarder

Precautions: If you do not complete the Lab Challenge exercise, you must still complete the Lab Cleanup steps prior to continuing on to Lab 5.

Delete the secondary zone that has been configured on the W2K8*xx* and W2K8*yy* servers. On the W2K8*xx* server, configure a DNS forwarder to the W2K8*yy* server, and then confirm that name resolution for both domains is still successful from W2K8*xx*. On the W2K8*yy* server, configure a conditional forwarder for the contoso.com domain to the W2K*xx* server, and then confirm that name resolution for both domains is still successful from W2K8*yy*.

LAB CLEANUP

Completion time   15 minutes

You have completed testing of the DNS server role, and now need to reset your Windows Server 2008 computers to their original state prior to performing testing of additional infrastructure services that you are planning to deploy to your production network.

After completing this exercise, you will know how to:

▲ Remove the DNS Server role

PART A: REMOVING THE DNS SERVER ROLE FROM W2K8*XX*

1.   Log on to the W2K8*xx* server. If the Server Manager console does not appear automatically, click the Start button, and then click Server Manager.

2.   In the left-hand pane of Server Manager, click Roles. In the right-hand pane, click Remove Roles. Click Next

3.   The Remove Server Roles screen appears. Remove the checkmark next to DNS Server, and then click Next.

4.   Click Remove, and then click Close when the removal has completed.

5.   When prompted, reboot the W2K8*xx* computer.

6.   Log on to the W2K8*xx* server after it reboots. The Server Manager console will reappear automatically. Click Finish when prompted.

7.   Log off of the W2K8*xx* server.

PART B: REMOVING THE DNS SERVER ROLE FROM W2K8*YY*

1. Log on to the W2K8*yy* computer. If Server Manager does not appear automatically, click the Start button, and then click Server Manager.

2. In the left-hand pane of Server Manager, click Roles. In the right-hand pane, click Remove Roles. Click Next

3. The Remove Server Roles screen appears. Remove the checkmark next to DNS Server, and then click Next.

4. Click Remove, and then click Close when the removal has completed.

5. When prompted, reboot the W2K8*yy* computer.

6. Log on to the W2K8*yy* server after it reboots. The Server Manager console will reappear automatically. Click Finish when prompted.

PART C: REMOVING THE DNS SERVER ROLE FROM CORE*XX*

1. Log on to the CORE*xx* server. From the command prompt, key **start /w ocsetup DNS-Server-Core-Role /uninstall**, and press Enter.

2. When prompted, click Yes to restart the server.

LAB 5.1
CONFIGURING FILE SERVICES

This lab contains the following exercises and activities:

BEFORE YOU BEGIN

Lab 5.1 assumes that setup has been completed as specified in the setup document and that your computer has connectivity to other lab computers and the Internet. The required exercises in Lab 5.1 assume that you have completed the preparatory exercises in Labs 1.1 and 1.2. Lab Challenge Exercise 5.1.2 assumes that you have completed the optional Server Core exercises in Labs 1.1 and 1.2.

The instructor PC is preconfigured as a domain controller in the lucernepublishing.com domain for demonstration purposes and is named INSTRUCTOR01.

> **NOTE**
>
> *In this lab manual, you will see the characters xx, yy, and zz. These directions assume that you are working on computers configured in pairs and that each computer has a number. One number is odd, and the other number is even. For example, W2K801 is the odd-numbered computer, and W2K802 is the even-numbered computer. When you see xx, substitute the unique number assigned to the odd-numbered computer. When you see yy, substitute the unique number assigned to the even-numbered computer. When you see zz, substitute the number assigned to the computer that you are working at, either odd or even.*

The four Windows Server 2008 server computers referenced in this lab will each be configured with static IP addresses. For ease of reference, record the static IP addresses of each server that you will be working with in this lab:

INSTRUCTOR01 (Instructor Computer)

IP Address: ___.___.___.___

Subnet Mask: ___.___.___.___

Default Gateway: ___.___.___.___

W2K8*xx*: (For example: W2K801)

IP Address: ___.___.___.___

Subnet Mask: ___.___.___.___

Default Gateway: ___.___.___.___

W2K8*yy*: (For example: W2K802)

IP Address: ___.___.___.___

Subnet Mask: ___.___.___.___

Default Gateway: ___.___.___.___

CORE*xx*: (For example: CORE01)

IP Address: ___.___.___.___

Subnet Mask: ___.___.___.___

Default Gateway: ___.___.___.___

SCENARIO

You are a network administrator for Lucerne Publishing. Recently, Lucerne Publishing has opened a new office in an adjacent building that has been connected to the existing Lucerne Publishing network. Now that network connectivity has been established, the staff in the new office will require storage for their mission-critical files and databases. Additionally, certain files need to be made available in both offices to users in each location.

After completing this lab, you will be able to:

■ Install the File Server Resource Manager

■ Create and Manage Windows File Shares

■ Configure DFS Namespaces and DFS-Replication

Estimated lab time: 155 minutes

Exercise 5.1.1	Installing the File Server Resource Manager
Overview	You have just procured multiple servers to act as file servers within your organization. You must prepare these servers to host Distributed File System (DFS) and other advanced functionality available in Windows Server 2008 file servers.
Outcomes	After completing this exercise, you will know how to: ▲ Install the File Server Resource Manager
Completion time	20 minutes
Precautions	This exercise will be performed on both the odd-numbered W2K8*xx* computer and the even-numbered W2K8*yy* computer.

1. Press Ctrl+Alt+Delete on the W2K8*zz* Windows Server 2008 computer assigned to you, and log on as the default administrator of the local computer. Your username will be Administrator. The password will be MSPress#1 or the password that your instructor or lab proctor assigns to you.

2. If the Initial Configuration Tasks (ICT) screen window opens automatically, place a checkmark next to Do not show this window at logon, and click Close.

3. If the Server Manager window does not appear automatically, click the Start button, and then click Server Manager.

4. In the left-hand pane of Server Manager, double-click Roles.

5. Click Add Roles. Click Next to bypass the initial Welcome screen.

6. The Select Server Roles screen appears. Place a checkmark next to File Services. Click Next twice to continue.

7. The Select Role Services screen appears. Confirm that there is a checkmark next to File Server. Place a checkmark next to each of the following, and then click Next:

    - Distributed File System

    - DFS-Namespaces

    - DFS-Replication

    - File Server Resource Manager

8. The Create a DFS Namespace screen appears. Select the Create a namespace later using the DFS Management Snap-In in Server Manager radio button. Click Next.

9. The Configure Storage Usage Monitoring screen appears. Place a checkmark next to Local Disk (C:).

Question 1	What reports does this screen generate by default?

10. Click Next. The Set Report Options screen appears.

Question 2	Where are reports stored by default?

11. Click Next, and then click Install. Click Close when the installation completes.

12. Log off of the W2K8*zz* computer.

Exercise 5.1.2	Creating and Managing Windows File Shares
Overview	You have configured two new Windows Server 2008 computers to act as file servers for the new Lucerne Publishing office. You will now configure multiple shared folders, also known as file shares, to test access levels for local users on each computer.
Outcomes	After completing this exercise, you will know how to: ▲ Create local users and groups ▲ Create and manage file shares
Completion time	25 minutes
Precautions	This exercise will be completed using both the even- and odd-numbered computers. Portions will be completed from the odd-numbered computer only; other portions will be completed from the even-numbered computer only.

■ PART A: CREATING LOCAL USERS AND GROUPS ON BOTH W2K8*ZZ* COMPUTERS

1. Log on to the W2K8*xx* computer. Click the Start button, followed by Administrative Tools, followed by Computer Management.

2. Drill down to Local Users and Groups→Users.

3. Right-click Users, and click New User…. Create a new user with the following information:

    - Username: **W2K8***zz***Test01**

    - Password: **MSPress#1**

    - Remove the "User must change password…" option

4. Create a second user with a username of W2K8*zz*Test02.

5. Right-click Groups, and click New Group…. Create a new group with the following information:

    - Group Name: **W2K8***zz***TestGroup01**

    - Members: **W2K8***zz***Test01**

6. Create a second group with a group name of **W2K8zzTestGroup02**, with **W2K8zzTest02** as a member.

7. Log off of the W2K8zz computer.

■ PART B: CONFIGURING FILE SHARES AND PERMISSIONS ON BOTH W2K8ZZ COMPUTERS

1. Log on to the W2K8zz computer as Administrator.

2. Create the following directories in the root of the C:\ drive:

    - C:\TestFolder01

    - C:\TestFolder02

    - C:\TestFolder03

    - C:\TestFolder04

3. Create an empty text file in each folder corresponding to the name of the folder: TestFile01.txt in C:\TestFolder01, TestFile02.txt in C:\TestFolder02, and so forth.

4. Right-click C:\TestFolder01, and click Share....

5. The File Sharing window appears. In the Choose people to share with text box, enter **W2K8zzTest01**. Click Add.

Question 3	*What is the access level granted to the newly added user?*

6. Click the drop-down box next to Reader.

Question 4	*What are the available access levels that can be granted?*

7. Click Contributor.

8. Click Share. If the Network discovery and file sharing window appears asking whether you want to enable network discovery for all public networks, click No, make the network that I am connected to a private network.

Question 5	What is the UNC path of the newly created share?

9. Click Done.

10. Repeat Steps 4 through 9 to share the TestFolder02 folder. Grant W2K8zzTest02 Contributor permissions to the share.

11. Repeat Steps 4 through 9 to share the TestFolder03 folder. Grant W2K8zzTestGroup01 Contributor permissions to the share.

12. Repeat Steps 4 through 9 to share the TestFolder04 folder. Grant W2K8zzTestGroup2 Contributor permissions to the share.

Question 6	What are the UNC paths of all shares configured on both servers?

■ PART C: CONFIRMING FILE SHARE ACCESS

1. Log on to the W2K8zz computer as the local Administrator.

2. Click Start, enter the UNC name of the other computer, and press Enter. For example, if you are logged on to the W2K802 computer, browse to \\W2K801. If you are logged on to the W2K801 computer, browse to \\W2K802.

Use between Parent & Child Server

3. Attempt to browse the contents of the shares on your partner's computer.

Question 7	Why is the local user from one computer able to access resources on the other computer?

4. Log off of the W2K8zz computer.

5. Log on to the W2K8zz computer as W2K8zzTest01.

6. Click Start, and then enter the UNC name of your partner's computer. For example, if you are logged on to the W2K802 computer, browse to \\W2K801. If you are logged on to the W2K801 computer, browse to \\W2K802.

Question 8	Why are you now prompted for a username and password?

7. Enter the username and password of W2K8zzTest01 for your partner's computer. For example, if you are attempting to access a share on W2K801, enter the credentials for W2K801Test01. Do *not* select the option to remember these credentials.

8. Attempt to access each shared folder using the W2K8zzTest01credentials.

Question 9	Which folders are you able to access and why??

9. Log off of the W2K8zz computer.

10. Log on to the W2K8zz computer as W2K8zzTest02.

11. Click Start, and then enter the UNC name of the other computer. For example, if you are logged on to the W2K802 computer, browse to \\W2K801. If you are logged on to the W2K801 computer, browse to \\W2K802.

12. Enter the username and password of W2K8zzTest02 for your partner's computer. For example, if you are attempting to access a share on W2K801, enter the credentials for W2K801Test02. Do *not* select the option to remember these credentials.

13. Attempt to access each shared folder using the W2K8zzTest01credentials.

Question 10	Which folders are you able to access?

14. Log off of the W2K8zz computer.

Exercise 5.1.3	Configuring DFS-Namespaces
Overview	Management has expressed a concern that Lucerne Publishing users will have difficulty locating individual files and folders as new servers are added to the network and has asked whether there is any mechanism to simplify this process. You decide to configure a DFS Namespace on the two Windows Server 2008 file servers to test the use of this function to create a single unified namespace for file and folder access.
Outcomes	After completing this exercise, you will know how to: ▲ Configure a DFS Namespace
Completion time	25 minutes
Precautions	This exercise will be performed on the odd-numbered W2K8*xx* computer only.

■ PART A: CONFIGURING A DFS NAMESPACE ON W2K801

1. Press Ctrl-Alt-Delete on the W2K8*xx* odd-numbered computer assigned to you, and log on as the default administrator of the local computer. Your username will be Administrator. The password will be MSPress#1 or the password that your instructor or lab proctor assigns to you.

2. Click Start→Administrative Tools→DFS Management.

3. Click Namespaces in the left-hand pane.

4. Right-click Namespaces, and click New Namespace....

5. The Namespace Server screen appears. In the Server: text box, enter **W2K801**, and click Next.

Question 11	*What message do you receive?*

6. Click Yes. The Namespace Name and Settings screen appears.

7. In the Name: text box, enter **Public**.

8.   Click Edit Settings.

Question 12	*What is the local path of the shared folder?*

Question 13	*What are the default shared folder permissions?*

9.   Click OK, and then click Next.

10. The Namespace Type screen appears. Accept the default selection, and click Next, followed by Create. Click Close when the namespace creation is completed.

11. Right-click the newly created namespace, and click New Folder....

12. The New Folder screen appears. In the Name: folder, enter **Folder01**. Click Add.

13. The Add Folder Target screen appears. In the Path to folder target: text box, enter **\\W2K8xx\TestFolder01**. Click OK twice.

14. Repeat Steps 11 through 13 to add the remaining shared folders to the DFS Namespace under the name Folder02, Folder03, and Folder04.

15. Log off of the W2K801xx computer.

■ PART B: CONFIRMING DFS-NAMESPACE FUNCTIONALITY

1.   Log on to the W2K8yy computer as W2K8yyTest01.

2.   Browse to \\W2K8xx\Public. When prompted, enter the username and password for W2K8xxTest01.

3.   Attempt to access each shared folder using the W2K8xxTest01 credentials.

Question 14	*Which folders are you able to access?*

4. Log off of the W2K8*yy* computer.

5. Log on to the W2K8*yy* computer as W2K8*yy*Test02.

6. Browse to \\W2K8*xx*\Public. When prompted, enter the username and password for W2K8*xx*Test02.

7. Attempt to access each shared folder using the W2K8*xx*Test02 credentials.

Question 15	Which folders are you able to access?

8. Log off of the W2K8*yy* computer.

Exercise 5.1.4	Configuring DFS-Replication
Overview	One of the Lucerne Publishing departments maintains offices in both building locations. This office needs to have certain files and folders accessible in both locations, and any changes made in each location must be reflected for users in the other location. You decide to configure a DFS replication group to test the functionality of the DFS-Replication role service in Windows Server 2008.
Outcomes	After completing this exercise, you will know how to: ▲ Configure a DFS-Replication replication group
Completion time	25 minutes
Precautions	This exercise will be performed on both the odd-numbered W2K8*xx* computer and the even-numbered W2K8*yy* computer.

■ PART A: JOINING THE W2K8*ZZ* COMPUTERS TO AN ACTIVE DIRECTORY DOMAIN

1. Log on to the W2K8*zz* computer as the local Administrator.

2. Click Start→Administrative Tools→Server Manager. In the Server Summary→Computer Information section, click Change System Properties.

3.   The System Properties screen appears.

Question 16	*What is this computer's current domain/workgroup configuration?*

4.   Click Change. The computer Name/Domain Changes screen appears.

5.   Click the Domain radio button. Key **lucernepublishing.com**, and then click OK.

6.   The Windows Security screen appears. Enter the username and password of an administrator in the lucernepublishing.com domain as provided by your instructor or lab proctor, and click OK. The Welcome to the lucernepublishing.com domain screen appears. Click OK twice.

7.   Click Close. When prompted, restart the computer.

■ PART B: CREATING FOLDERS TO BE CONFIGURED FOR DFS REPLICATION ON EACH COMPUTER

1.   Log on to the W2K8*zz* computer as the Administrator for the lucernepublishing domain.

2.   Create a folder in the root of the C:\ drive called Replication. Share this folder as \\W2K8*zz*\Replication. Click the drop-down arrow, and then click Find. Grant the Domain Users group from the lucernepublishing.com domain the Co-owner share permission.

3.   Log off of the W2K8*zz* computer.

■ PART C: CONFIGURING DFS REPLICATION ON THE ODD-NUMBERED COMPUTER

1.   Log on to the W2K8*xx* odd-numbered computer as an administrator of the lucernepublishing.com domain.

2.   Click Start→Administrative Tools→DFS Management.

3.   Right-click Replication, and then click New Replication Group....

4. The Replication Group Type screen appears.

Question 17	What types of preconfigured replication groups can you configure?

5. Click Next. The Name and Domain screen appears. In the Name of replication group: text box, enter **DFSReplication**.

6. Click Next.

7. The Replication Group Members screen appears. Click Add.

8. The Select Computers screen appears. Enter the name of the odd-numbered computer, and then click OK.

9. Click Add. The Select Computers screen appears again. Enter the name of the even-numbered computer, and then click OK.

10. The Topology Selection screen appears.

Question 18	Why is the hub-and-spoke topology grayed out?

11. Click Next. The Replication Group Schedule and Bandwidth screen appears. Accept the default selection, and click Next.

12. The Primary Member screen appears. In the Primary member: drop-down box, select the odd-numbered W2K8*xx* computer.

13. Click Next. The Folders to Replicate screen appears. Click Add, and specify the C:\Replication folder created in PART B.

14. Click OK, and then click Next. The Local Path of Replication on Other Members screen appears.

Question 19	What member server and local path are configured?

15. Click Edit. Set the status of the even-numbered computer to Enabled, and specify the Local path as C:\Replication.

16. Click OK, followed by Next, followed by Create.

17. Click OK. The Replication Delay screen appears. Read the warning message, and then click OK.

■ PART D: TESTING THE FUNCTIONALITY OF DFS REPLICATION

1. Open the C:\Replication folder on the W2K8*xx* computer. Create a blank text file called TestReplication.txt.

2. Log off of the odd-numbered computer.

3. Log on to the even-numbered computer as the local administrator.

4. Open the C:\Replication folder on the even-numbered computer. Confirm that the TestReplication.txt file appears.

NOTE	*If the file does not appear immediately, wait a few minutes, and refresh the Windows Explorer screen.*

5. Modify the TestReplication.txt file on the even-numbered computer.

6. Log off of the even-numbered computer.

7. Log on to the odd-numbered computer as the local administrator.

8. Open the C:\Replication\TestReplication.txt file from the odd-numbered computer.

9. Confirm that the changes to the TestReplication.txt file that you made in Step 5 appear.

NOTE	*If the file modifications do not appear immediately, close the file, wait a few minutes, refresh the Windows Explorer screen, and check again.*

10. Log off of the even-numbered computer.

LAB REVIEW QUESTIONS

Completion time	15 minutes

1. In your own words, describe what you learned by completing this lab.

2. When completing Exercise 5.1.3, where was the configuration information for the \\W2K8*xx*\Public namespace stored?

3. You are configuring DFS-Replication between two offices that share a heavily utilized WAN connection and are concerned that DFS-R replication traffic will overwhelm the link. What feature of DFS-R in Windows Server 2008 can help to minimize the impact of replication over a WAN link?

4. What mechanism will be used by the Public namespace to provide DFS referrals outside of a client's site? What other mechanisms are available?

LAB CHALLENGE 5-1-1: CONFIGURING A FILE SCREEN

Completion time	15 minutes

Lucerne Publishing management has expressed a concern that users will take up too much room on the new file servers by storing personal files, such as MP3 music files. You want to test the file screen functionality in the File Server Resource Manager to determine whether this can help prevent the issue from occurring.

After completing this exercise, you will know how to:

▲ Configure a file screen in Windows Server 2008

Precautions: If you do not complete the Lab Challenge exercises, you must still complete the Lab Cleanup steps prior to continuing on to Lab 5.2.

Configure a file screen on the odd-numbered computer to prevent users from saving files with a .MP3 file extension.

NOTE	*You can test the functionality of this File Screen by creating a text file and manually assigning it a ".mp3" file extension.*

LAB CHALLENGE 5-1-2: CONFIGURING FILE SHARES ON A SERVER CORE COMPUTER

Completion time	15 minutes

To increase the security of servers deployed in several additional remote offices, you have prepared servers running the Windows Server 2008 Server Core installation option to provide infrastructure services to these offices. You must now prepare one of these servers to function as a file server.

After completing this exercise, you will know how to:

▲ Configure file shares from the Windows command line

Precautions: If you do not complete the Lab Challenge exercises, you must still complete the Lab Cleanup steps prior to continuing on to Lab 5.2.

Log on to the CORE*xx* computer. Create and configure local user accounts and file shares from the Windows command line. (*Hint: key **net** /? at the command prompt to get started.*) Test access to these file shares from a remote computer to confirm the functionality of these shares.

LAB CLEANUP

Completion time	15 minutes

You have completed testing of the File Services server role and now need to reset your Windows Server 2008 computers to their original state prior to performing testing of additional infrastructure services that you are planning to deploy to your production network.

After completing this exercise, you will know how to:

▲ Remove the File Services server role

■ PART A: DELETING THE DFS NAMESPACE AND DFS REPLICATION GROUP ON W2K8*XX*

1.   Log on to the W2K8*xx* computer as the administrator of lucernepublishing.com.

2.   Click Start→Administrative Tools→DFS Management.

3.   Expand Namespaces in the left-hand pane.

4.   Right-click W2K8*xx*\Public, and click Delete.

5. The Confirm Delete Namespace screen appears. Select the Yes, delete the namespace and all its folders radio button, and click OK.

6. Click Replication in the left-hand pane.

7. Right-click DFSReplication, and click Delete.

8. The Confirm Delete Replication Group screen appears. Select the Yes, delete the replication group, stop replicating all associated replicated folders, and delete all members of the replication group, and click OK.

■ PART B: DELETING ALL SHARED FILES AND FOLDERS ON W2K8*ZZ* AND CORE*XX*

1. Using Windows Explorer, un-share and delete all shared folders that you have configured on the odd- and even-numbered computers.

NOTE	*You may need to reboot both computers after removing the DFS Namespace and DFS Replication group before you will be able to delete the files and folders.*

2. Delete the C:\DFSRoots folder from the odd-numbered computer.

3. Using the Computer Management MMC snap-in, delete any local users and groups that you have created on the W2K8*zz* computer.

4. Using the Windows command-line, un-share and delete all shared folders, users, and groups that you have configured on the CORE*xx* Server Core computer.

■ PART C: REMOVING THE FILE SERVICES SERVER ROLE FROM W2K8*ZZ*

1. Log on to the W2K8*zz* server. If the Server Manager console does not appear automatically, click the Start button, and then click Server Manager.

2. In the left-hand pane of Server Manager, click Roles. In the right-hand pane, click Remove Roles. Click Next.

3. The Remove Server Roles screen appears. Remove the checkmark next to File Services, and then click Next.

4. Click Remove, and then click Close when the removal has completed.

5. When prompted, reboot the W2K8*xx* computer.

6. Log on to the W2K8*zz* server after it reboots. The Server Manager console will reappear automatically. Click Finish when prompted.

7. Log off of the W2K8*zz* server.

■ PART D: DISJOINING THE W2K8*ZZ* COMPUTER FROM THE LUCERNEPUBLISHING.COM DOMAIN

1. Log on to the W2K8*zz* computer. If Server Manager does not appear automatically, click the Start button, and then click Server Manager.

2. In the right-hand pane of Server Manager, click Change System Properties.

3. The System Properties screen appears. On the Computer Name tab, click Change. In the Member of: section, click the Workgroup radio button, and enter **WORKGROUP** as the workgroup name.

4. Click OK three times, followed by Close.

5. Reboot the computer when prompted.

LAB 5.2
CONFIGURING PRINT SERVICES

This lab contains the following exercises and activities:

Exercise 5.2.1	Installing the Print Server Role
Exercise 5.2.2	Creating and Managing Windows Printers
Exercise 5.2.3	Installing the Internet Printing Protocol
Lab Review	Questions
Lab Challenge	Publishing Printers in Active Directory Using Group Policy
Lab Cleanup	

BEFORE YOU BEGIN

Lab 5.2 assumes that setup has been completed as specified in the setup document and that your computer has connectivity to other lab computers and the Internet. The required exercises in Lab 5.2 assume that you have completed the preparatory exercises in Labs 1.1 and 1.2.

The instructor PC is preconfigured as a domain controller in the lucernepublishing.com domain for demonstration purposes and is named INSTRUCTOR01.

> | | *In this lab manual, you will see the characters xx, yy, and zz. These directions assume that you are working on computers configured in pairs and that each computer has a number. One number is odd, and the other number is even. For example, W2K801 is the odd-numbered computer, and W2K802 is the even-numbered computer. When you see xx, substitute the unique number assigned to the odd-numbered computer. When you see yy, substitute the unique number assigned to the even-numbered computer. When you see zz, substitute the number assigned to the computer that you are working at, either odd or even.* |
> | :-: | :-- |
> | **NOTE** | |

The four Windows Server 2008 server computers referenced in this lab will each be configured with static IP addresses. For ease of reference, record the static IP addresses of each server that you will be working with in this lab:

INSTRUCTOR01 (Instructor Computer)

IP Address: ___.___.___.___

Subnet Mask: ___.___.___.___

Default Gateway: ___.___.___.___

W2K8*xx*: (For example: W2K801)

IP Address: ___.___.___.___

Subnet Mask: ___.___.___.___

Default Gateway: ___.___.___.___

W2K8*yy*: (For example: W2K802)

IP Address: ___.___.___.___

Subnet Mask: ___.___.___.___

Default Gateway: ___.___.___.___

CORE*xx*: (For example: CORE01)

IP Address: ___.___.___.___

Subnet Mask: ___.___.___.___

Default Gateway: ___.___.___.___

SCENARIO

You are a network administrator for Lucerne Publishing. Recently, Lucerne Publishing has opened a new office in an adjacent building that has been connected to the existing Lucerne Publishing network. Now that network connectivity has been established and file sharing capabilities have been tested and deployed, the staff in the new office will require the ability to print documents to local and network-attached printers.

After completing this lab, you will be able to:

- Install the Print Server Role

- Create and manage Windows printers

- Install the Internet Printing Protocol

Estimated lab time: 130 minutes

Exercise 5.2.1	Installing the Print Server Role
Overview	You have just procured multiple servers to act as print servers within your organization. You must prepare these servers to host the Print Server Role within your organization.
Outcomes	After completing this exercise, you will know how to: ▲ Install the Print Server role
Completion time	20 minutes
Precautions	If working in pairs, this exercise can be performed on both the odd-numbered W2K8*xx* computer and the even-numbered W2K8*yy* computer. If working alone, this exercise can be performed on the odd-numbered W2K8*xx* computer only.

1. Press Ctrl+Alt+Delete on the W2K8*zz* Windows Server 2008 computer assigned to you, and log on as the default administrator of the local computer. Your username will be Administrator. The password will be MSPress#1 or the password that your instructor or lab proctor assigns to you.

2. If the Initial Configuration Tasks (ICT) screen window opens automatically, place a checkmark next to Do not show this window at logon, and click Close.

3. If the Server Manager window does not appear automatically, click the Start button, and then click Server Manager.

4. In the left-hand pane of Server Manager, double-click Roles.

5.   Click Add Roles. Click Next to dismiss the initial Welcome screen.

6.   The Select Server Roles screen appears. Place a checkmark next to Print Services. Click Next twice to continue.

7.   The Select Role Services screen appears. Confirm that there is a checkmark next to Print Server.

8.   Click Next, and then click Install. When the Print Services role installation finishes, click Close.

9.   Log off of the W2K8zz computer.

Exercise 5.2.2	Creating and Managing Windows Printers
Overview	You have configured two new Windows Server 2008 computers to act as print servers for the new Lucerne Publishing office. You will now configure multiple printers and printer drivers to test the functionality of Windows Server 2008 Print Services.
Outcomes	After completing this exercise, you will know how to: ▲ Install printer drivers ▲ Install printers
Completion time	25 minutes
Precautions	This exercise will be completed using both the even- and odd-numbered computers.

■ PART A: MANAGING PRINTER DRIVERS

1.   Log on to the W2K8zz computer. Click the Start button, followed by Administrative Tools, followed by Print Management.

2.   Drill down to Print Servers→W2K8zz (local).

3.   Right-click Drivers, and click Add Driver....

4.   The Add Printer Driver Wizard screen appears. Click Next.

5.   The Processor and Operating System Selection screen appears.

Question 1	*What processor types are listed?*

Question 2	What processor type(s) are selected by default?

6. Click Next. The Printer Driver Selection screen appears.

7. In the Manufacturer column, click HP. In the Printers column, click HP LaserJet 4.

8. Click Next, and then clickFinish.

■ PART B: ADDING A LOCAL PRINTER

1. Right-click Printers, and click Add Printer....

2. The Printer Installation screen appears.

Question 3	What installation methods are available?

3. Select the Add a new printer using an existing port radio button. Select LPT1: (Printer Port) in the drop-down box.

4. Click Next. The Printer Driver screen appears.

5. Click the Use an existing printer driver on the computer radio button. Select HP LaserJet 4 in the drop-down box.

6. Click Next. The Printer Name and Sharing Settings screen appears.

7. Accept the default settings.

8. Click Next twice, followed by Finish.

■ PART C: CREATING A PRINTER POOL

1. Right-click Printers, and click Add Printer....

2. The Printer Installation screen appears.

3. Select the Add a new printer using an existing port radio button. Select LPT2: (Printer Port) in the drop-down box.

4.   Click Next. The Printer Driver screen appears.

5.   Click the Use an existing printer driver on the computer radio button. Select HP LaserJet 4 in the drop-down box.

6.   Click Next. The Printer Name and Sharing Settings screen appears.

7.   Accept the default settings.

8.   Click Next twice, and then click Finish.

9.   Double-click Printers in the left-hand pane. Right-click HP LaserJet 4, and select Properties.

10.   Select the Ports tab. Place a checkmark next to Enable Printer Pooling.

11.   Place a checkmark next to LPT2:, and click OK.

■ PART D: CONFIRMING PRINTER SECURITY SETTINGS.

1.   Double-click Printers in the left-hand pane. Right-click HP LaserJet 4, and click Properties.

2.   Select the Security tab.

Question 4	*What are the default security settings for the printer?*

■ PART E: CUSTOMIZING PRINTER SETTINGS

1.   Select the Advanced tab.

2.   Select the Available from: radio button, and set the printer schedule so that it is available from 8am to 5pm.

Question 5	*What is the printer's default priority?*

3.   Click Cancel. Log off of the W2K8*zz* computer.

Exercise 5.2.3	Installing the Internet Printing Protocol
Overview	The Lucerne Publishing IT department has decided to test the functionality of Web-based printing in Windows Server 2008 for the newly opened office. You need to install the Internet Printing Protocol (IPP) on two Windows Server 2008 computers that you are using to test print server functionality.
Outcomes	After completing this exercise, you will know how to: ▲ Install and configure the Internet Printing Protocol (IPP)
Completion time	25 minutes
Precautions	If students are working in pairs, this exercise will be completed using both the even- and odd-numbered computers. If students are working alone, this exercise can be performed on the odd-numbered W2K8*xx* computer only.

■ PART A: DISABLING ENHANCED INTERNET SECURITY

1. Press Ctrl+Alt+Delete on the W2K8*zz* computer assigned to you, and log on as the default administrator of the local computer. Your username will be Administrator. The password will be MSPress#1 or the password that your instructor or lab proctor assigns to you.

2. Click Start→Server Manager. In the right-hand pane, scroll to the Security Information section. Click Configure IE ESC.

3. The Internet Explorer Enhanced Security Configuration window appears. In the Administrators section, select the Off radio button, and click OK.

■ PART B: INSTALLING THE INTERNET PRINTING PROTOCOL

1. Click Start→Server Manager. Click the plus sign (+) next to Roles.

2. Right-click Print Services, and click Add Role Services.

3. The Select Role Services screen appears. Place a checkmark next to Internet Printing.

4. The Add Role Services screen appears.

Question 6	*What roles must be added to enable Internet Printing?*

5.   Click Add Required Role Services.

6.   Click Next three times, and then click Install.

7.   When the installation completes, click Close.

■ PART C: CONFIRMING THE FUNCTIONALITY OF INTERNET PRINTING ON THE LOCAL COMPUTER

1.   Click the Start button. Key **http://w2k8zz/printers**.

2.   The Connect to W2K8zz screen appears. Enter the administrator username and password for W2K8zz, and click OK.

3.   The Microsoft Phishing Filter screen appears. Click the Turn on Automatic Phishing Filter (recommended) radio button, and click OK.

4.   If the Do You See The Information Bar? screen appears, place a checkmark next to Don't show this message again, and click OK.

5.   If the Information Bar reads "Intranet settings are now turned off by default. Intranet settings are less secure than Internet settings. Click here for more options…," click the Information Bar, and select Enable Intranet Settings. Click Yes to confirm.

Question 7	*What is the name of the Web page that is displayed?*

6.   Click HP Laserjet 4.

Question 8	*What commands are listed in the left-hand column?*

LAB REVIEW QUESTIONS

Completion time	15 minutes

1. In your own words, describe what you learned by completing this lab.

2. What is the difference between the Manage Printers permission and the Manage Documents permission?

3. What is the difference between EMF, PCL, and XPS?

LAB CHALLENGE: PUBLISHING PRINTERS IN ACTIVE DIRECTORY USING GROUP POLICY

Completion time	30 minutes

Once you have completed testing of the Windows Server 2008 print server functionality, you wish to start deploying printers automatically via Group Policy Objects within the Lucerne Publishing Active Directory domain.

After completing this exercise, you will know how to:

▲ Deploy printers via Group Policy

Working with your instructor, join the W2K8*zz* and VISTA*xx* computers to the Lucerne Publishing Active Directory domain. Create a Group Policy Object that will deploy the HP LaserJet 4 printer to the Domain Users group in Active Directory.

> **NOTE** *Your instructor has already created one or more test user accounts in a test Organizational Unit (OU) and has created a sample GPO to help you test this functionality.*

LAB CLEANUP

Completion time	15 minutes

You have completed testing of the Print Services server role and now need to reset your Windows Server 2008 computers to their original state prior to performing testing of additional infrastructure services that you are planning to deploy to your production network.

After completing this exercise, you will know how to:

▲ Remove the Print Services server role

■ PART A: DELETING SHARED PRINTERS FROM W2K8*ZZ*

1. Log on to the W2K8*zz* computer as the administrator of lucernepublishing.com.

2. Click Start→Administrative Tools→Print Management.

3. Expand Print Servers→W2K8*zz* (local)→Printers in the left-hand pane.

4. Right-click HP LaserJet 4, and click Delete. Click Yes to confirm.

5. Right-click HP LaserJet 4 (Copy 1), and click Delete. Click Yes to confirm.

6. Close the Print Management Console.

■ PART B: REMOVING THE PRINT SERVICES ROLE

1. Click the Start button, and then click Server Manager.

2. Click the plus sign next to Roles. Right-click Roles, and then click Remove Roles.

3. Click Next. The Remove Server Roles screen appears.

4. Remove the checkmark next to Print Services and Web Server (IIS).

5. Click Next. Confirm that the Delete printers installed on the server radio button is selected.

6. Click Next, and then click Remove.

7. Click Close, and then click Yes to reboot the server.

8. When the computer reboots, log on as the administrator of the lucernepublishing.com domain. Click Close when the Remove Roles Wizard appears.

9. Log off of the W2K8*zz* computer.

■ PART C (IF LAB CHALLENGE WAS COMPLETED): DISJOINING THE W2K8ZZ COMPUTER FROM THE LUCERNEPUBLISHING.COM DOMAIN

1. Log on to the W2K8*zz* computer. If Server Manager does not appear automatically, click the Start button, and then click Server Manager.

2. In the right-hand pane of Server Manager, click Change System Properties.

3. The System Properties screen appears. On the Computer Name tab, click Change. In the Member of: section, click the Workgroup radio button, and enter **WORKGROUP** as the workgroup name.

4. Click OK three times, followed by Close.

5. Reboot the computer when prompted.

LAB 5.3
USING FILE AND PRINT SERVICES

This lab contains the following exercises and activities:

BEFORE YOU BEGIN

The classroom network consists of Windows Server 2008 student servers that are all connected to a local area network. There is also a classroom server, named ServerDC, that is connected to the same classroom network. ServerDC is also running Windows Server 2008 and is the domain controller for a domain named contoso.com. Throughout the labs in this manual, you will be working with the same student server on which you will install, configure, maintain, and troubleshoot application roles, features, and services.

Your instructor should have supplied you with the information needed to fill in the following table:

Student computer name (Server##)	
Student account name (Student##)	

To complete the exercises in this lab, you will require access to a second student computer on the classroom network, referred to in the exercises as your *partner server*. Depending on the configuration of your network, use one of the following options as directed by your instructor:

- For a conventional classroom network with one operating system installed on each computer, you must have a lab partner with his or her own computer, performing the same exercises as yourself.

- For a classroom in which each computer uses local virtualization software to install multiple operating systems, you must run two virtual machines representing student computers and perform the exercises separately on each virtual machine.

- For a classroom that uses online virtualization, you will have access to two virtual student servers in your Web browser. You must perform the exercises separately on each virtual machine.

Working with Lab Worksheets

Each lab in this manual requires that you answer questions, shoot screen shots, or perform other activities that you are to document in a worksheet named for the lab, such as lab01_worksheet. Your instructor will supply you with the worksheet files by copying them to the Students\Worksheets share on ServerDC. As you perform the exercises in each lab, open the appropriate worksheet file using WordPad, fill in the required information, and save the file to your computer's Student##\Documents folder. This folder is automatically redirected to the ServerDC computer. Your instructor will examine these worksheet files to assess your performance.

The procedure for opening and saving a worksheet file is as follows:

1. Click Start, and then click Run. The Run dialog box appears.

2. In the Open text box, key **\\ServerDC\Students\Worksheets\lab##_worksheet** (where lab## contains the number of the lab you're completing), and click OK.

3. The worksheet document opens in Wordpad.

4. Complete all of the exercises in the worksheet.

5.   In WordPad, choose Save As from the File menu. The Save As dialog box appears.

6.   In the File Name text box, key **lab##_worksheet_*yourname*** (where lab## contains the number of the lab you're completing and *yourname* is your last name), and click Save.

SCENARIO

You are an administrator for Contoso, Ltd., assigned to the test lab. Your supervisor has instructed you to demonstrate the capabilities of the file and print services included with Windows Server 2008.

After completing this lab, you will be able to:

■   Install the File Services and Print Services roles

■   Create and manage a DFS namespace

■   Install a printer

■   Deploy printers in Active Directory

Estimated lab time: 130 minutes

Exercise 5.3.1	Installing the File and Print Services Roles
Overview	In this exercise, you prepare your lab server for the demonstration by installing the roles that implement advanced file and print tools in Windows Server 2008.
Completion time	10 minutes

1.   Turn on your computer. When the logon screen appears, log on using your Student## account and the password *P@ssw0rd*.

2.   Close the Initial Configuration Tasks window when it appears.

3.   Click Start, point to Administrative Tools, and click Server Manager. Click Continue in the User Account Control message box, and the Server Manager console appears.

4.   Select the Roles node, and click Add Roles. The Add Roles Wizard appears, displaying the *Before You Begin* page.

5.   Click Next to continue. The *Select Server Roles* page appears.

NOTE

If your computer already has other roles installed, remove them before you proceed with this lab.

6. Select the File Services and Print Services checkboxes, and click Next. The *Introduction to Print Services* page appears.

7. Click Next to bypass the introductory page. The *Select Role Services* page appears, as shown in Figure 5-3-1.

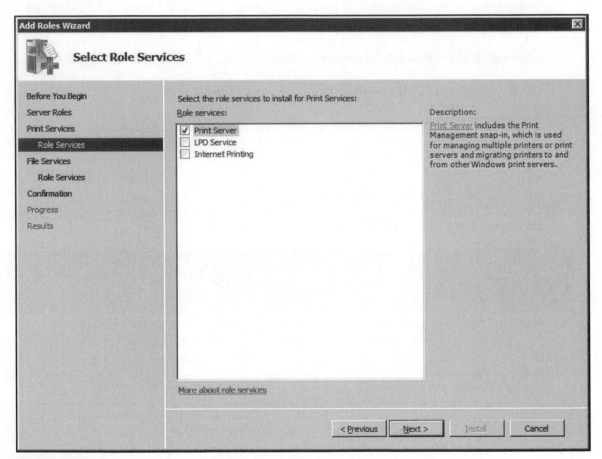

Figure 5-3-1
Select Role Services page for the Print Services role

8. Click Next to accept the default Print Server role service. The *Introduction to File Services* page appears.

9. Click Next to bypass the introductory page. The *Select Role Services* page appears, as shown in Figure 5-3-2.

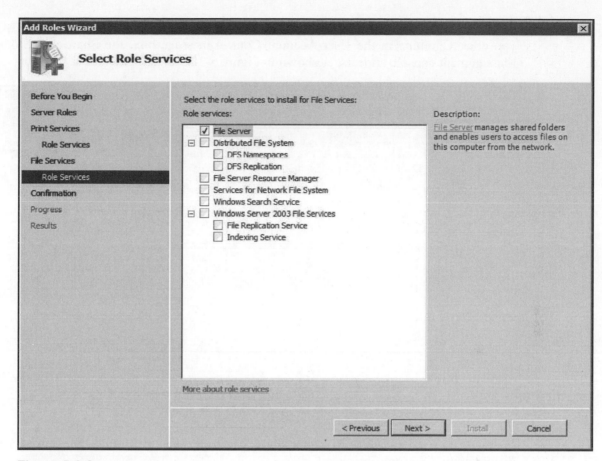

Figure 5-3-2
Select Role Services page for the File Services role

10. Select the Distributed File System role service, and click Next. The *Create a DFS Namespace* page appears.

11. Select the Create a namespace later using the DFS Management snap-in in Server Manager option, and click Next. The *Confirm Installation Selections* page appears.

12. Click Install. The wizard installs the roles, and the *Installation Results* page appears.

13. Click Close.

14. Close the Server Manager console, and leave the computer logged on for the next exercise.

Exercise 5.3.2	Creating a Volume Using Share and Storage Management
Overview	In this exercise you demonstrate the ability to provision storage in the new Share and Storage Management console in Windows Server 2008.
Completion time	10 minutes

1. Click Start, and then click Administrative Tools > Share and Storage Management. After you click Continue in the User Account Control message box, the Share and Storage Management console appears, as shown in Figure 5-3-3.

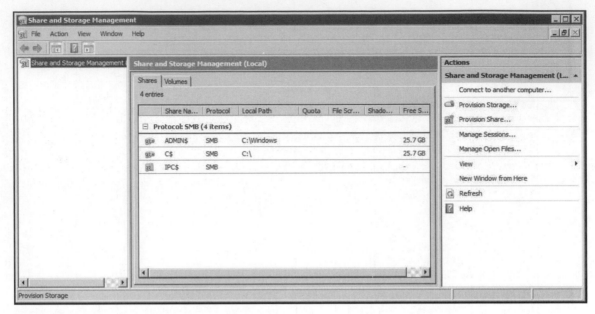

Figure 5-3-3
Share and Storage Management console

2. In the actions pane, click Provision Storage. The Provision Storage Wizard appears, displaying the *Storage Source* page.

3. Click Next to accept the default One or more disks available on this server option. The *Disk Drive* page appears.

4. Select Disk 1, and click Next. The *Volume Size* page appears.

> **NOTE**
>
> *If Disk 1 does not appear in the Provision Storage Wizard, open the Computer Management console, select the Disk Management snap-in, and make sure that Disk 1 is initialized.*

5. In the Specify a size for the new volume spin box, select a value that represents half the total size of Disk 1, and then click Next. The *Volume Creation* page appears.

6. Leave the Assign drive letter to this volume option selected. From the drop-down list, select the drive letter X, and then click Next. The *Format* page appears.

7. Leave the Format volume checkbox selected and, in the Volume label text box, key **Docs**. Leave the other settings at their defaults, and click Next. The *Review Settings And Create Storage* page appears.

8. Click Create. The wizard creates and formats the volume.

9. Click Close.

10. Press Ctrl+Prt Scr to take a screen shot of the Volumes tab in the Share and Storage Management console, showing the volume you just created, and then press Ctrl+V to paste the resulting image into the lab05_3_worksheet file in the page provided.

11. Leave the Sharing and Storage Management console open for the next exercise.

Exercise 5.3.3	Creating a Share Using Share and Storage Management
Overview	In this exercise, you demonstrate the ability to create and manage shares in the Share and Storage Management console in Windows Server 2008.
Completion time	10 minutes

1. In the Sharing and Storage Management console, click Provision Share. The Provision A Shared Folder Wizard appears, displaying the *Shared Folder Location* page.

2. Click Browse. The Browse For Folder dialog box appears.

3. Select the x$ share, and click Make New Folder. Key **Docs**, and click OK. The x:\Docs path appears in the Location text box.

4. Click Next. The *NTFS Permissions* page appears.

5. Select the Yes, change NTFS permissions option, and click Edit Permissions. The Permissions for Docs dialog box appears.

> **NOTE**
>
> *The share administration policies in your company call for all access control to be performed using NTFS permissions, not share permissions.*

6. Click Add. The Select Users, Computers, or Groups dialog box appears.

7. In the Enter the object names to select box, key **Students; Domain Admins**, and click OK. The two security principals appear in the Group or user names list.

8. Select the Domain Admins group. In the Permissions for Domain Admins box, select the Allow Full Control checkbox, and then click Apply.

9. Select the Students group. In the Permissions for Students box, select the Allow Write and Allow Modify checkboxes, and then click Apply.

10. Press Ctrl+Prt Scr to take a screen shot of the Permissions for Docs dialog box, showing the NTFS permissions assigned to the Students group, and then press Ctrl+V to paste the resulting image into the lab05_3_worksheet file in the page provided.

11. Click OK to close the Permissions for Docs dialog box.

12. Click Next. The *Share Protocols* page appears.

13. Leave the SMB checkbox selected. In the Share Name text box, key **Documents**, and then click Next. The *SMB Settings* page appears.

14. Click Advanced. The Advanced dialog box appears.

15. Select the Enable access-based enumeration checkbox, and click OK.

16. Click Next. The *SMB Permissions* page appears.

17. Select the Users and groups have custom share permissions option, and click Permissions. The Permissions for Documents dialog box appears.

18. Select Everyone. In the Permissions for Everyone box, select Allow Full Control, and then click OK.

19. Click Next. The *DFS Namespace Publishing* page appears.

20. Click Next. The *Review Settings And Create Share* page appears.

21. Click Create. The wizard creates the share.

22. Click Close.

23. Press Ctrl+Prt Scr to take a screen shot of the Share and Storage Management console, showing the share you just created, and then press Ctrl+V to paste the resulting image into the lab05_3_worksheet file in the page provided.

24. Close the Share and Storage Management console.

25. Leave the computer logged on for the next exercise.

Exercise 5.3.4	Creating a DFS Namespace
Overview	In this exercise, you use the Distributed File System role service to create a DFS namespace that takes advantage of Active Directory Domain Services.
Completion time	10 minutes

1. Click Start, and then click Administrative Tools > DFS Management. Click Continue in the User Account Control message box, and the DFS Management console appears, as shown in Figure 5-3-4.

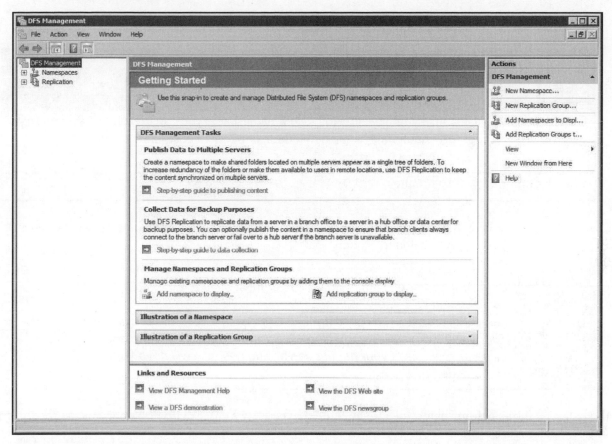

Figure 5-3-4
DFS Management console

2. Select the Namespaces node and, in the actions pane, click New Namespace. The New Namespace Wizard appears, displaying the *Namespace Server* page.

3. In the Server text box, key **Server##**, where ## is the number assigned to your server, and click Next. The *Namespace Name And Settings* page appears.

4. In the Name text box, key **Docs##**, where ## is the number assigned to your computer.

5. Click Edit Settings. The Edit Settings dialog box appears.

6. Select the Administrators have full access; other users have read and write permissions option, and click OK. Then click Next. The *Namespace Type* page appears.

7. Leave the Domain-based namespace option selected, and click Next. The *Review Settings and Create Namespace* page appears.

8. Click Create. The wizard creates the namespace.

9. Click Close. The Docs## namespace appears in the DFS Management console.

10. Leave the DFS Management console open for the next exercise.

Exercise 5.3.5	Adding a Folder to a Namespace
Overview	Once you have created a DFS namespace, you can add shared folders from any computer on the network, making them accessible through the namespace.
Completion time	10 minutes

1. In the DFS Management console, expand the Namespaces node, and select the Docs## namespace you created in Exercise 5.3.4.

> **NOTE**
>
> *Both your server and your partner server must have Exercise 5.3.4 completed in its entirety, with each server having its own DFS namespace, before you continue with Exercise 5.3.5. At the conclusion of Exercise 5.3.5, your server will have your partner server's share added to its namespace, and your partner server's namespace will have your share added to it.*

2. In the actions pane, select New Folder. The New Folder dialog box appears, as shown in Figure 5-3-5.

3. In the Name text box, key **Server ## Documents**.

4. Click Add. The Add Folder Target dialog box appears.

5. In the Path to folder target text box, key **\\Server##\Documents**, and click OK twice. The folder appears in the namespace.

6. Click New Folder to open the New Folder dialog box again.

7. Click Add to open the Add Folder Target dialog box.

8. Click Browse. The Browse for Shared Folders dialog box appears.

9. In the Server text box, key **Server##**, where ## is the number assigned to your partner server, and click Show Shared Folders.

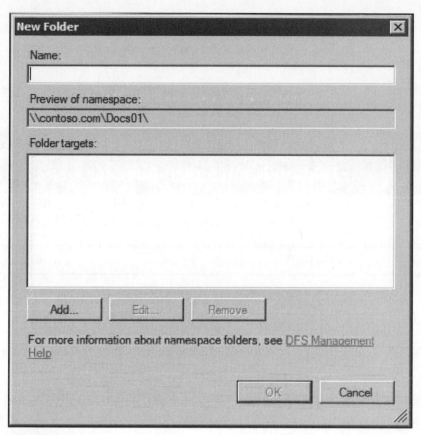

Figure 5-3-5
New Folder dialog box

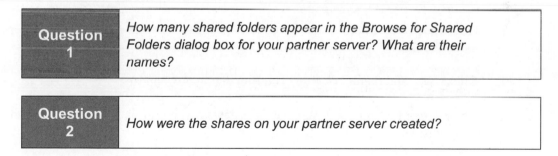

Question 1	How many shared folders appear in the Browse for Shared Folders dialog box for your partner server? What are their names?

Question 2	How were the shares on your partner server created?

10. Select the Documents share, and click OK. The path to the share appears in the Add Folder Target dialog box.

11. Click OK. The share appears in the New Folder dialog box.

12. In the Name text box, key **Server## Documents**, where ## is the number assigned to your partner server, and then click OK. The new folder appears on the Namespace tab in the console.

13. Press Ctrl+Prt Scr to take a screen shot of the DFS Management console, showing both of the shared folders in your namespace, and then press Ctrl+V to paste the resulting image into the lab05_3_worksheet file in the page provided.

Question 3	On this domain-based namespace, where are the files stored that appear in the two Server## Documents folders?

14. Close the DFS Management console, and leave the computer logged on for the next exercise.

Exercise 5.3.6	Testing Namespace Access
Overview	To test a DFS namespace, you access it by using the server name and the name you specified during the namespace creation process.
Completion time	10 minutes

1. Open Windows Explorer, and browse to the X:\Docs folder you created in Exercise 5.3.3.

2. Right-click anywhere in the detail (right) pane and, from the context menu, select New > Folder.

3. Key **Statistics##**, where ## is the number assigned to your computer, and press Enter to name the folder.

4. Select the folder you created in the scope (left) pane, right-click anywhere in the detail pane and, from the context menu, select New > Rich Text Document.

5. Key **Budget##**, where ## is the number assigned to your computer, and press Enter to name the file.

6. Click Start, and then click Run. The Run dialog box appears.

7. In the Open text box, key **\\Server##\Docs##**, where ## is the number assigned to your partner server.

8. Click OK. An Explorer window appears, displaying the DFS namespace on your partner server.

Question 4	How many folders appear in the namespace?

9. Press Ctrl+Prt Scr to take a screen shot of the Explorer window, showing the namespace on your partner server and its folders, and then press Ctrl+V to paste the resulting image into the lab05_3_worksheet file in the page provided.

10. Open the Server## Documents folder named for your server, expand the Statistics folder, and double-click the Budget file to open it in Wordpad.

11. Key your name into the Budget file, and click File > Save.

Question 5	Which computer is hosting the DFS namspace you are currently accessing?

Question 6	On which computer are you saving the modified version of the Budget file?

12. In Windows Explorer, open the C:\DfsRoots\Docs## folder.

13. Double-click the Server## Documents folder, named for your partner server.

Question 7	What happens?

14. Double-click the Server## Documents folder, named for your own server.

Question 8	What happens this time?

Question 9	How can you explain these results?

15. Close the two Explorer windows, and leave the server logged on for the next exercise.

Exercise 5.3.7	Adding a Namespace Server
Overview	One of the advantages of a domain-based DFS namespace is the ability to designate multiple namespace servers for fault tolerance purposes.
Completion time	10 minutes

1. Open the Run dialog box. In the Open text box, key **\\contoso.com\Docs##**, where ## is the number assigned to your server, and then click OK. An Explorer window appears, displaying the Docs## namespace you created.

Question 10	Where are the target folders for this namespace, which you are seeing in the Explorer window, currently being stored?

2. Shut down your partner server for a few minutes (or ask your lab partner to shut it down).

NOTE	During this exercise, if you are working with a lab partner, you will have to take turns shutting down your servers momentarily and using each other's servers to access your namespaces.

3. Try to open the two Server## Documents folders on your Docs## namespace.

Question 11	How is access to your Docs## namespace impaired while your partner server is shut down?

4. Start up your partner server again, and shut down your own server.

5. At your partner server, log on using your Student## account and the password *P@ssw0rd*.

6. Try to access your Docs## namespace by opening the \\contoso.com\Docs## path from the Run dialog box.

Question 12	How is access to your Docs## namespace affected while your server is shut down?

7. Log off of your partner server, and restart your own server.

8. Log on to your server using your Student## account and the password *P@ssw0rd*.

9. Open the DFS Management console, and expand the Namespaces node.

10. Select the Docs## namespace you created in Exercise 5.3.4 and, in the actions pane, click Add Namespace Server. The Add Namespace Server dialog box appears, as shown in Figure 5-3-6.

11. In the Namespace server text box, key the name of your partner server, **Server##**.

12. Click Edit Settings. The Edit Settings dialog box appears.

13. Select the Administrators have full access; other users have read and write permissions option, and click OK. Then, in the Add Namespace Server dialog box, click OK again.

14. In the DFS Management console, select the Namespace Servers tab.

15. Press Ctrl+Prt Scr to take a screen shot of the DFS Management console, showing the two namespace servers in your Docs## namespace, and then press Ctrl+V to paste the resulting image into the lab05_3_worksheet file in the page provided.

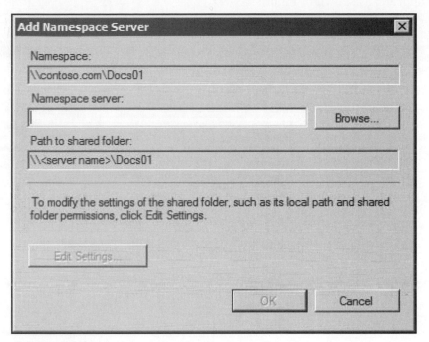

Figure 5-3-6
Add Namespace Server dialog box

16. Shut down your server, and try again to access the two folders in your Docs## namespace from your partner server.

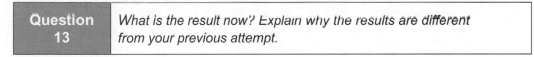

Question 13	*What is the result now? Explain why the results are different from your previous attempt.*

17. Restart your server.

Exercise 5.3.8	**Installing a Printer**
Overview	On your test network, you are examining the capabilities of the Print Management console included in Windows Server 2008. In this exercise, you use the Print Management console to install some test printers.
Completion time	10 minutes

1. Log on using your Student## account and the password *P@ssw0rd*.

2. Close the Initial Configuration Tasks window when it appears.

3. Click Start, and then click Administrative Tools > Print Management. After you click Continue in the User Account Control message box, the Print Management console appears, as shown in Figure 5-3-7.

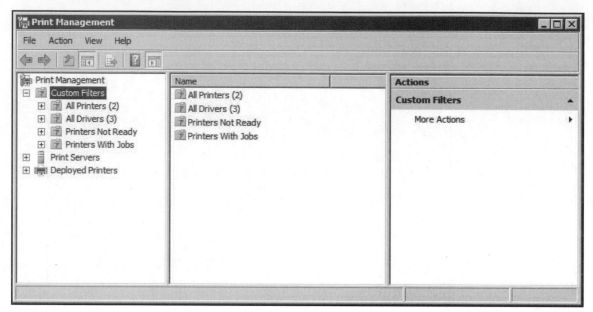

Figure 5-3-7
Print Management console

4. Expand the Print Servers node, and then right-click the Server## (local) node, representing your computer. From the context menu, select Add Printer. The Network Printer Installation Wizard appears.

5. Select the Add a new printer using an existing port option. Leave the LPT1: (Printer Port) value selected, and then click Next. The *Printer Driver* page appears.

6. Leave the Install a new driver option selected, and click Next. The *Printer Installation* page appears.

7. In the Manufacturer list, select Generic.

8. In the Printers list, select MS Publisher Color Printer, and click Next. The *Printer Name and Sharing Settings* page appears.

9. In the Printer Name text box, key **MSColor##**, where ## is the number assigned to your computer.

10. Leave the Share this printer checkbox selected. In the Share Name text box, key **MSColor##**, and then click Next. The *Printer Found* page appears.

Question 14	Is the wizard able to determine whether the printer you selected is actually connected to the computer? Why or why not?

11. Click Next. The *Completing the Network Printer Installation Wizard* page appears.

12. Once the printer is installed, click Finish.

13. Repeat the process to install a second printer, using the following settings:

   - Port: LPT2
   - Manufacturer: Generic
   - Printer: MS Publisher Imagesetter
   - Printer Name: MSMono##, where ## is the number assigned to your computer
   - Share Name: MSMono##, where ## is the number assigned to your computer

14. Select the Printers node under your particular print server in the Print Management console.

15. Press Ctrl+Prt Scr to take a screen shot of the Print Management console, showing the contents of the Printers node, and then press Ctrl+V to paste the resulting image into the lab05_worksheet file in the page provided.

16. Leave the Print Management console open for the next exercise.

Exercise 5.3.9	Deploying Printers Using Active Directory
Overview	To simplify future network printer deployments, your company plans to publish printer connections using Active Directory and Group Policy. In this execise, you deploy the printers you created in two different ways.
Completion time	10 minutes

1. In the Print Management console, expand the node representing your server, and select the Printers node beneath it.

2. Right-click the MSColor## printer and, from the context menu, select List In Directory.

3. Right-click the MSMono## printer and, from the context menu, select Deploy with Group Policy. The Deploy with Group Policy dialog box appears, as shown in Figure 5-3-8.

4. Click Browse. The Browse For A Group Policy Object dialog box appears.

5.   Select Default Domain Policy, and click OK. Default Domain Policy appears in the GPO Name field.

6.   Select the The computers that this GPO applies to (per machine) checkbox, and click Add.

7.   Click OK. A Print Management message box appears, indicating that the printer deployment has succeeded.

8.   Click OK to close the message box, and click OK again to close the Deploy with Group Policy dialog box.

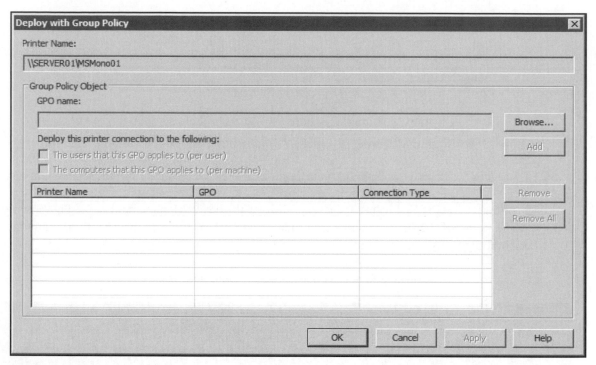

Figure 5-3-8
Deploy with Group Policy dialog box

9.   When this exercise is completed to this point on your partner server, restart your computer.

10.   When your computer restarts, log on using your Student## account and the password *P@ssw0rd*.

11.   Click Start, and then click Control Panel.

12.   Double-click the Printers icon. The Printers window appears.

Question 15	Apart from Microsoft XPS Document Writer, which appears by default, which of your partner server's printers appear in the window?

Question 16	Why doesn't your partner server's MSColor## printer appear in the Printers window?

13. Click Start, and then click Network. The Network window appears.

14. Click Search Active Directory. The Find Users, Contacts, and Groups dialog box appears.

15. In the Find drop-down list, select Printers. The title of the dialog box changes to Find Printers.

16. Click Find Now.

Question 17	What printers appear in the Search Results box?

17. Right-click your partner server's MSColor## printer and, from the context menu, select Connect.

18. Switch to the Printers window.

Question 18	What has changed in the Printers window?

19. Press Ctrl+Prt Scr to take a screen shot of the Printers window, and then press Ctrl+V to paste the resulting image into the lab05_worksheet file in the page provided.

20. Close the Printers window and the Network window.

21. Log off of the computer.

LAB REVIEW QUESTIONS

Completion time	10 minutes

1. In Exercise 5.3.2, you used the Sharing and Storage Management console to create a simple volume. What must you do to create a different volume type such as a mirrored, striped, or RAID-5 volume?

2. In Exercise 5.3.7, you accessed a DFS namespace using the Contoso domain name. One reason for creating a domain-based namespace instead of a standalone namespace is to suppress the server name in the namespace path. Why is suppressing the server name considered an advantage?

3. In Exercise 5.3.6, you accessed the DFS namespace on your partner server and modified a file called Budget. Explain why the file you modified was actually stored on your own server and not the partner server.

4. In Exercise 5.3.4 when you created a domain-based namespace, the Enable Windows Server 2008 mode checkbox on the *Namespace Type* page was selected by default. Under what circumstances would this checkbox be grayed out?

LAB CHALLENGE: CONFIGURING DFS REPLICATION

Completion time	20 minutes

In Exercise 5.3.7, you added a second namespace server to your domain-based namespace so that if one of the servers fails, the namespace still remains available. However, even though the namespace would remain available in the event of a server failure, one of the shared folders in the namespace would not be available. To make the data folders in the namespace fault tolerant as well, you can use DFS Replication to duplicate each folder on the other server.

To complete this challenge, use the DFS Management console to configure your Docs## namespace to be fully fault tolerant by using DFS Replication so that all resources remain available when one of the two servers fails. List the steps for the procedure you use to configure the namespace. Press Ctrl+Prt Scr to take a screen shot of the DFS Management console, demonstrating that the Docs## namespace is using DFS Replication, and then press Ctrl+V to paste the resulting image into the lab05_3_worksheet file in the page provided.

> **NOTE**
> *To avoid conflicts with your partner server, do not use the same folder name when replicating your folders to the other server. For example, if you were replicating a folder called Data01 to your partner server, you might call the folder Data01a.*

WORKSTATION RESET: RETURNING TO BASELINE

Completion time	10 minutes

To return the computer to its baseline state, complete the following procedures.

1. Open the DFS Management console, and delete the Docs## namespace you created, along with its folders.

2. Open the Share and Storage Management console, and delete the Documents share you created.

3. Open the Server Manager console, and remove the File Services and Print Services roles as well as the installed printers.

LAB 6.1
MANAGING SERVERS

This lab contains the following exercises and activities:

Exercise 6.1.1   Creating an MMC Console

Exercise 6.1.2   Using Remote Desktop

Exercise 6.1.3   Installing the Web Server (IIS) Role

Exercise 6.1.4   Installing WSUS

Exercise 6.1.5   Configuring WSUS

Exercise 6.1.6   Using the WSUS Administrator Console

Lab Review   Questions

Lab Challenge   Configuring Automatic Updates

Workstation Reset   Returning to Baseline

BEFORE YOU BEGIN

The classroom network consists of Windows Server 2008 student servers that are all connected to a local area network. There is also a classroom server, named ServerDC, that is connected to the same classroom network. ServerDC is also running Windows Server 2008 and is the domain controller for a domain named contoso.com. Throughout the labs in this manual, you will be working with the same student server on which you will install, configure, maintain, and troubleshoot application roles, features, and services.

Your instructor should have supplied you with the information needed to fill in the following table:

Student computer name (Server##)	
Student account name (Student##)	

To complete the exercises in this lab, you will require access to a second student computer on the classroom network, referred to in the exercises as your *partner server*. Depending on the configuration of your network, use one of the following options as directed by your instructor:

- For a conventional classroom network with one operating system installed on each computer, you must have a lab partner with his or her own computer, performing the same exercises as yourself.

- For a classroom in which each computer uses local virtualization software to install multiple operating systems, you must run two virtual machines representing student computers and perform the exercises separately on each virtual machine.

- For a classroom that uses online virtualization, you will have access to two virtual student servers in your Web browser. You must perform the exercises separately on each virtual machine.

Working with Lab Worksheets

Each lab in this manual requires that you answer questions, shoot screen shots, or perform other activities that you are to document in a worksheet named for the lab, such as lab01_worksheet. Your instructor will supply you with the worksheet files by copying them to the Students\Worksheets share on ServerDC. As you perform the exercises in each lab, open the appropriate worksheet file using WordPad, fill in the required information, and save the file to your computer's Student##\Documents folder. This folder is automatically redirected to the ServerDC computer. Your instructor will examine these worksheet files to assess your performance.

The procedure for opening and saving a worksheet file is as follows:

1. Click Start, and then click Run. The Run dialog box appears.

2. In the Open text box, key **\\ServerDC\Students\Worksheets\lab##_worksheet** (where lab## contains the number of the lab you're completing), and click OK.

3. The worksheet document opens in WordPad.

4. Complete all of the exercises in the worksheet.

5. In WordPad, choose Save As from the File menu. The Save As dialog box appears.

6. In the File Name text box, key **lab##_worksheet_*yourname*** (where lab## contains the number of the lab you're completing and *yourname* is your last name), and click Save.

SCENARIO

Your assignment today in your company's network test lab is to train some entry-level IT technicians in basic server management practices. To do this, you are going to demonstrate how to use tools such as Microsoft Management Console, Remote Desktop, and Windows Server Update Services.

After completing this lab, you will be able to:

- Create a custom MMC console

- Use Remote Desktop to connect to another computer

- Install, configure, and use Windows Server Update Services

Estimated lab time: 110 minutes

Exercise 6.1.1	Creating an MMC Console
Overview	In this exercise, you create a custom MMC console that will enable the IT staff to access all of the Active Directory domain administration tools in one console.
Completion time	10 minutes

1. Turn on your computer. When the logon screen appears, log on to the domain with your Student## account, where ## is the number assigned by your instructor, using the password *P@ssw0rd*.

2. Click Start, and then click Run. The Run dialog box appears.

3. In the Open text box, key **mmc**, and click OK. Click Continue in the User Account Control message box, and a blank Microsoft Management Console window appears, as shown in Figure 6-1-1.

4. Click File > Add/Remove Snap-in. The Add or Remove Snap-ins dialog box appears.

5. In the Available Snap-ins list, select Active Directory Domains and Trusts, and click Add.

6. In the Available Snap-ins list, select Active Directory Sites and Services, and click Add.

7. In the Available Snap-ins list, select Active Directory Users and Computers, and click Add.

8. In the Available Snap-ins list, select Group Policy Management, and click Add.

9.   Click OK. The snap-ins you selected appear in the console window.

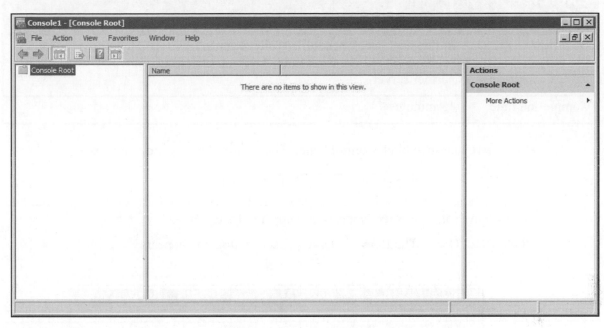

Figure 6-1-1
Microsoft Management Console window

10.   Click File > Options. The Options dialog box appears.

11.   In the text box at the top of the dialog box, key **Contoso.com Domain Tools**.

12.   In the Console mode drop-down list, select User mode – full access.

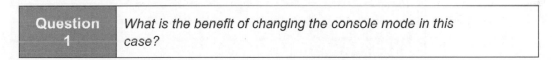

Question 1	*What is the benefit of changing the console mode in this case?*

13.   Select the Do not save changes to this console checkbox.

14.   Clear the Allow the user to customize views checkbox, and click OK.

15.   Expand each of the four snap-ins you added to the console.

16.   Press Ctrl+Prt Scr to take a screen shot of the Contoso.com Domain Tools console, and then press Ctrl+V to paste the resulting image into the lab06_1_worksheet file in the page provided.

17.   Click File > Save As. The Save As combo box appears.

18.   Save the file to your Student##\Documents folder, using the name **Student##_domain_tools**.

19.   Leave the computer logged on for the next exercise.

Exercise 6.1.2	Using Remote Desktop
Overview	In this exercise, you configure the Remote Desktop capabilities of your server and then use the Remote Desktop Connection client to access your partner server.
Completion time	15 minutes

1.   Click Start, and then click Control Panel. The Control Panel window appears.

2.   Double-click System. The System control panel appears.

3.   Click Remote Settings. Click Continue in the User Account Control message box, and the System Properties sheet appears, as shown in Figure 6-1-2.

4.   Click Select Users. The Remote Desktop Users dialog box appears.

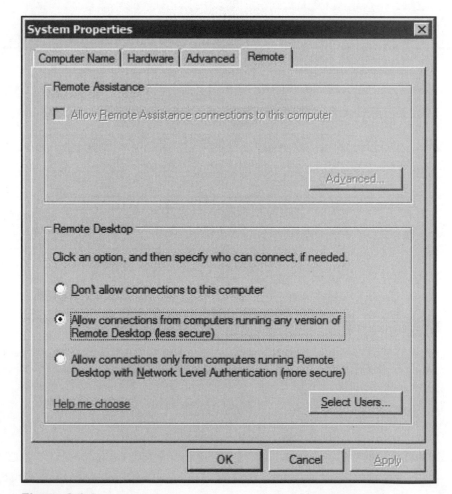

Figure 6-1-2
System Properties sheet

5. Click Add. The *Select Users or Groups* page appears.

6. In the Enter the object names to select text box, key **Students**, and click OK. The Students group appears in the Remote Desktop Users dialog box.

7. Click OK to close the Remote Desktop Users dialog box.

8. Click OK to close the System Properties sheet.

9. Close the System control panel.

10. Click Start, and then click All Programs > Accessories > Remote Desktop Connection. The Remote Desktop Connection window appears.

11. Click Options. The Remote Desktop Connection window expands.

12. On the General tab in the Computer text box, key **Server##**, where ## is the number assigned to your partner server.

13. Click the Display tab, and set the Remote desktop size slider to a resolution smaller than that of your computer.

14. Click the Local Resources tab, and click the More button. The Local Devices and Resources dialog box appears.

15. Select the Drives checkbox, and click OK.

16. Click the Experience tab, and confirm that the Performance drop-down list is set to LAN (10 Mbps or higher).

17. Click Connect. A Remote Desktop Connection message box appears, asking whether you trust the remote connection.

> **NOTE** *Your partner server should be logged off before you proceed with the following steps.*

18. Click Connect. A Windows Security dialog box appears.

19. In the User Name text box, key **contoso\student##**, where ## is the number assigned to your computer.

20. In the Password text box, key **P@ssw0rd**, and click OK. A Server## - Remote Desktop window appears containing an image of the remote computer's desktop.

21. In the Server## - Remote Desktop window, minimize the Initial Configuration Tasks window.

22. In the Server## - Remote Desktop window, click Start, and then click Administrative Tools > Terminal Services > Terminal Services Manager.

23. Click Continue in the User Account Control message box, and the Terminal Services Manager console appears.

Question 2	Which computer is running the Microsoft Management Console program that is hosting the Terminal Services Manager snap-in?

24. In the detail pane on the Users tab, right-click the Student## session and, from the context menu, select Status. A Status of LogOn ID # dialog box appears.

25. Press Ctrl+Prt Scr to take a screen shot of the Server## - Remote Desktop window, and then press Ctrl+V to paste the resulting image into the Lab06_1_worksheet file in the page provided.

26. In the Server## - Remote Desktop window, click Close to close the Status of LogOn ID # dialog box.

27. In the Server## - Remote Desktop window, close the Terminal Services Manager window.

28. In the Server## - Remote Desktop window, Click Start. Click the right arrow button, and select Log Off. The Server## - Remote Desktop window closes.

29. Leave the computer logged on for the next exercise.

Exercise 6.1.3	Installing the Web Server (IIS) Role
Overview	In this exercise, you install the Web Server (IIS) role that Windows Software Update Services (WSUS) requires to provide updates to clients on the network.
Completion time	10 minutes

1. Click Start, and then click Administrative Tools > Server Manager. Click Continue in the User Account Control message box, and the Server Manager console appears.

2. Select the Roles node and, in the detail pane, click Add Roles. The Add Roles Wizard appears.

3. Click Next to bypass the *Before You Begin* page. The *Select Server Roles page* appears.

4. Select the Web Server (IIS) checkbox, and click Next. An Add Roles Wizard message box appears, listing the features that are required to add the Web Server (IIS) role.

5. Click Add Required Features, and then click Next. The *Introduction to Web Server (IIS)* page appears.

6. Click Next to bypass the introductory page. The *Select Role Services* page appears.

7. Select the ASP.NET checkbox. An Add Roles Wizard message box appears, listing the role services and features that are required to add the ASP.NET role service.

8. Click Add Required Role Services.

9. Select the Windows Authentication and IIS 6.0 Management Compatibility checkboxes, and click Next. The *Confirm Installation Selections* page appears.

10. Click Install. The wizard installs the role.

11. Click Close.

12. Close the Server Manager console.

13. Click Start, and then click Internet Explorer. An Internet Explorer window appears.

14. In the address box, key **http://server##**, where ## is the number assigned to your computer, and press Enter.

15. Press Ctrl+Prt Scr to take a screen shot of the Internet Explorer window, and then press Ctrl+V to paste the resulting image into the lab06_1_worksheet file in the page provided.

16. Close the Internet Explorer window.

17. Leave the computer logged on for the next exercise.

Exercise 6.1.4	Installing WSUS
Overview	In this exercise, you install the Windows Server Update Services software supplied by your instructor.
Completion time	10 minutes

1. Click Start, and then click Run. The Run dialog box appears.

2. In the Open text box, key **\\serverdc\install\wsus3.0sp1**, and click OK. A Windows Explorer window appears, displaying the contents of the \wsus3.0sp1 folder.

3. Double-click the ReportViewer file. Click Continue in the User Account Control message box, and the Microsoft Report Viewer Redistributable 2008 Setup Wizard appears.

4. Click Next to bypass the Welcome page. The *End-User License Agreement* page appears.

5. Select the I accept the terms of the License Agreement checkbox, and click Install. The wizard installs the software, and the *Setup Complete* page appears.

6. Click Finish. The wizard closes.

7. In the Windows Explorer window, double-click the WSUSSetup_30SP1_x86 file (or WSUSSetup_30SP1_x64, depending on which processor platform your computer is using). Click Continue in the User Account Control message box, and the Windows Server Update Services 3.0 SP1 Setup Wizard appears, as shown in Figure 6-1-3.

Figure 6-1-3
Windows Server Update Services 3.0 SP1 Setup Wizard

8. Click Next to bypass the Welcome page. The *Installation Mode Selection* page appears.

9. Leave the Full server installation including Administration Console option selected, and click Next. The *License Agreement* page appears.

10. Select *I accept the terms of the License agreement*, and click Next. The *Select Update Source* page appears.

11. Leave the Store updates locally checkbox selected. In the text box, key **C:\Updates**, and click Next. The *Database Options* page appears.

12. Click Next to accept the default settings. The *Web Site Selection* page appears.

13. Leave the Use the existing IIS Default Web site option selected, and click Next. The *Ready to Install Windows Server Update Services 3.0 SP1* page appears.

14. Click Next. The *Installing* page appears.

15. The wizard installs WSUS, and the *Completing the Windows Server Update Services 3.0 SP1 Setup Wizard* page appears.

16. Click Finish. The Windows Server Update Services 3.0 SP1 Setup Wizard closes, and the Windows Server Update Services Configuration Wizard appears.

17. Leave the computer logged on for the next exercise.

Exercise 6.1.5	Configuring WSUS
Overview	In this exercise, you configure the Windows Server Update Services software supplied by your instructor.
Completion time	10 minutes

1. In the Windows Server Update Services Configuration Wizard, click Next to bypass the *Before You Begin* page. The *Join the Microsoft Update Improvement Program* page appears.

2. Clear the Yes, I would like to join the Microsoft Update Improvement Program checkbox, and click Next. The *Choose Upstream Server* page appears.

3. Select the Synchronize from another Windows Server Update Services server option. In the Server name text box, key **ServerDC**, and click Next. The *Specify Proxy Server* page appears.

4. Click Next to accept the default settings. The *Connect To Upstream Server* page appears.

5. Click Start Connecting. The wizard connects to the Microsoft Update site and downloads a list of available updates.

6. Click Next. The *Choose Languages* page appears.

7. Click Next to accept the default settings. The *Choose Products* page appears.

8. Clear the Office checkbox and the Windows checkbox.

9. Select all of the Windows Server 2008 and Windows Vista checkboxes, as shown in Figure 6-1-4.

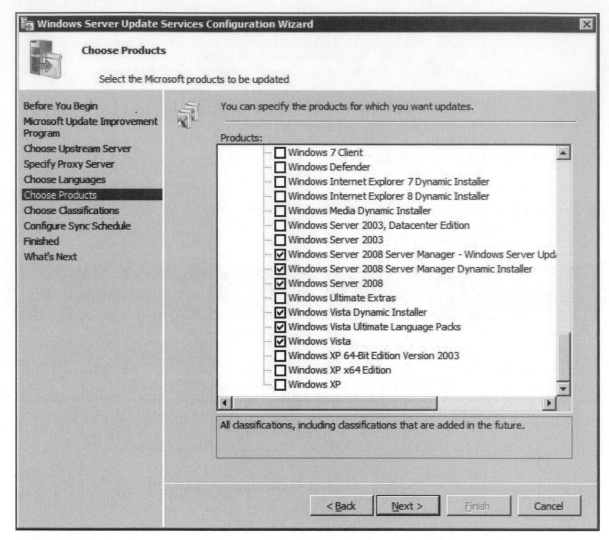

Figure 6-1-4
Choose Products page of the Windows Server Update Services Configuration Wizard

10. Click Next. The *Choose Classifications* page appears.

11. Click Next to accept the default selections. The *Set Sync Schedule* page appears.

12. Leave the Synchronize manually option selected, and click Next. The *Finished* page appears.

13. Clear the Launch the Windows Server Update Services Administration Console and Begin initial synchronization checkboxes, and click Next. The *What's Next* page appears.

14. Click Finish. The wizard closes.

15. Leave the computer logged on for the next exercise.

Exercise 6.1.6	Using the WSUS Administrator Console
Overview	In this exercise, you use the WSUS Administrator console to initiate a synchronization event that downloads updates to your server.
Completion time	15 minutes

1. Click Start, and then click Administrative Tools > Microsoft Windows Server Update Services 3.0 SP1. Click Continue in the User Account Control message box, and the Update Services console appears.

2. In the scope (left) pane, select the SERVER## node.

3. In the detail pane, click Synchronize now.

4. Wait for the synchronization process to finish. This could take several minutes depending on the speed of your connection.

Question 3	*How many critical and security updates did WSUS download?*

5. Press Ctrl+Prt Scr to take a screen shot of the Update Services console, and then press Ctrl+V to paste the resulting image into the lab06_1_worksheet file in the page provided.

6. In the scope pane, expand the SERVER## and Computers nodes.

7. Right-click All Computers and, from the context menu, select Add Computer Group. The Add Computer Group dialog box appears.

8. In the Name text box, key **Windows Server 2008 Servers**, and click Add. The new group appears under the All Computers node.

NOTE	*Please note that groups you create in the Update Services console are not in any way related to Active Directory groups or the computer's local groups.*

9. In the scope pane, select Options.

10. In the detail pane, select Computers. The Computers dialog box appears.

11. Select Use Group Policy or registry settings on computers, and click OK.

12. In the scope pane, expand the Updates node, and then select All Updates.

13. In the detail pane in the Status drop-down list, select Any. A list of the downloaded updates appears in the detail pane.

14. Click the Classification column head to resort the list.

15. Scroll down in the list of updates, and select the first Windows Server 2008 entry for your processing platform.

16. In the actions pane, click Approve. The Approve Updates dialog box appears.

17. Select the Windows Server 2008 Servers group, and click the down arrow. From the context menu, select Approved for Install, and then click OK. An Approval Progress dialog box appears.

Question 4	*What was the result of the approval process?*

18. Click Close.

19. Press Ctrl+Prt Scr to take a screen shot of the Update Services console, showing the list of updates, and then press Ctrl+V to paste the resulting image into the lab06_1_worksheet file in the page provided.

20. Repeat steps 15 to 18 to approve all of the Windows Server 2008 updates that appear in the list.

21. Close the Update Services console.

22. Close all open windows, and log off of the computer.

LAB REVIEW QUESTIONS

Completion time	10 minutes

1. In Exercise 6.1.2, you used the System Properties sheet to grant the Students group the ability to connect to your server using Remote Desktop. What is another way to do the same thing?

2. In Exercise 6.1.2, if you selected the Allow connections only from computers running Remote Desktop with Network Level Authentication option, which operating systems would not be able to connect to your server using Remote Desktop?

3. In Exercise 6.1.5, which settings would you change in the Windows Server Update Services Configuration Wizard if you wanted to configure a WSUS server in a branch office to download updates, configuration settings, and approvals from a WSUS server in the corporate headquarters?

LAB CHALLENGE: CONFIGURING AUTOMATIC UPDATES

Completion time	20 minutes

You have installed and configured Windows Server Update Services on your computer, and you have downloaded and approved all of the available updates for Windows Server 2008. To complete this challenge, you must create a Group Policy object that can configure client computers to join the Windows Server 2008 Servers group you created, access your WSUS server, and automatically download and install all available updates every Monday at 2:00 AM. Create a GPO named WSUS##, where ## is the number assigned to your computer, and configure all of the policies needed to achieve these goals. Press Ctrl+Prt Scr to take a screen shot of each policy you modify, showing the settings you configured, and then press Ctrl+V to paste the resulting image into the lab06_1_worksheet file in the page provided. Do not link the GPO to any Active Directory object.

WORKSTATION RESET: RETURNING TO BASELINE

Completion time	10 minutes

To return the computer to its baseline state, complete the following procedures.

1. Open the Server Manager console, and remove the Web Server (IIS) role.

2. Restart the server when you are prompted to do so.

3. Open the Server Manager console, and remove the Windows Process Activation Server feature.

4. Restart the server again when you are prompted to do so.

LAB 6.2
MAINTAINING AND UPDATING WINDOWS SERVER 2008

This lab contains the following exercises and activities:

BEFORE YOU BEGIN

Lab 6.2 assumes that setup has been completed as specified in the setup document and that your computer has connectivity to other lab computers and the Internet. The required exercises in Lab 6.2 assume that you have completed the preparatory exercises in Labs 1.1 and 1.2.

The instructor PC is preconfigured as a domain controller in the lucernepublishing.com domain for demonstration purposes, and it is named INSTRUCTOR01. Before completing Exercise 6.2.3, configure each computer to use the INSTRUCTOR01 computer as its preferred DNS server as described in Lab 1.1 and Lab 1.2.

NOTE	*In this lab manual, you will see the characters xx, yy, and zz. These directions assume that you are working on computers configured in pairs and that each computer has a number. One number is odd, and the other number is even. For example, W2K801 is the odd-numbered computer, and W2K802 is the even-numbered computer. When you see xx, substitute the unique number assigned to the odd-numbered computer. When you see yy, substitute the unique number assigned to the even-numbered computer. When you see zz, substitute the number assigned to the computer that you are working at, either odd or even.*

The four Windows Server 2008 server computers referenced in this lab will each be configured with static IP addresses. For ease of reference, record the static IP addresses of each server that you will be working with in this lab:

INSTRUCTOR01 (Instructor Computer)

IP Address: ___.___.___.___

Subnet Mask: ___.___.___.___

Default Gateway: ___.___.___.___

W2K8xx: (For example: W2K801)

IP Address: ___.___.___.___

Subnet Mask: ___.___.___.___

Default Gateway: ___.___.___.___

W2K8yy: (For example: W2K802)

IP Address: ___.___.___.___

Subnet Mask: ___.___.___.___

Default Gateway: ___.___.___.___

CORExx: (For example: CORE01)

IP Address: ___.___.___.___

Subnet Mask: ___.___.___.___

Default Gateway: ___.___.___.___

SCENARIO

You are a network administrator for Lucerne Publishing. Lucerne Publishing is in the process of deploying numerous Windows Server 2008 computers to several remote locations in order to provide infrasturcture services such as DHCP, DNS, and File and Print Services. In order to make provisions for future purchase decisions as well as maintaining ongoing operational efficiency, you now need to put a plan in place to monitor the performance of the Lucerne Publishing servers and network connectivity. Additionally, you wish to deploy a centralized solution to deploy security patches and updates to the Lucerne Publishing servers.

After completing this lab, you will be able to:

■ Use the Reliability and Performance Monitor

■ Use the Windows Event Viewer

■ Install and use the Windows Network Monitor

■ Install and configure WSUS

Estimated lab time: 180 minutes

Exercise 6.2.1	Using the Reliability and Performance Monitor
Overview	You have finished testing multiple servers to act as infrastructure servers within your organization. You will now test the Reliability and Performance Monitor functionality within Windows Server 2008.
Outcomes	After completing this exercise, you will know how to: ▲ Launch the Reliability and Performance Monitor ▲ Add counters to Performance Monitor ▲ View reports in Reliability Monitor
Completion time	20 minutes
Precautions	If students are working in pairs, this exercise should be performed on both the odd-numbered W2K8*xx* computer and the even-numbered W2K8*yy* computer. If students are working alone, this exercise can be performed on the odd-numbered W2K8*xx* computer only.

1. Press Ctrl+Alt+Delete on the W2K8*zz* Windows Server 2008 computer assigned to you, and log on as the default administrator of the local computer. Your username will be Administrator. The password will be MSPress#1 or the password that your instructor or lab proctor assigns to you.

2. If the Initial Configuration Tasks (ICT) screen window opens automatically, place a checkmark next to Do not show this window at logon, and click Close.

3. If the Server Manager window does not appear automatically, click the Start button, and then click Server Manager.

4. In the left-hand pane of Server Manager, expand Diagnostics.

5. Expand Reliability and Performance, and then expand Monitoring Tools.

Question 1	What headings are available in the right-hand pane?

6. Click Performance Monitor in the left-hand pane.

7. Click the green plus-sign toolbar button in the middle pane. The Add Counters screen appears.

8. Click the plus sign next to Processor in the Available Counters section. In the lower left-hand corner of the Add Counters screen, place a checkmark next to Show description.

9. Click % Idle Time.

Question 2	What is monitored by % Idle time? *% Idle time is the % of time the processor is idle during the sample interval*
Question 3	What instances are available in the Instances of selected object section?

10. Click Total, and then click Add. Click OK.

11. Click the % Idle Time line in the legend underneath the graph.

Question 4	What is the average value of % Idle Time on the W2K8zz computer? *93.9*

12. Click the green plus sign in the middle pane. The Add Counters screen appears.

13. Click the plus sign next to System in the Available Counters section.

14. Click Processor Queue Length, and then click Add.
15. Click OK. Click the Processor Queue Length line in the middle pane.

Question 5	*What is the average value of Processor Queue Length on the W2K8zz computer?*

16. Click Reliability Monitor in the left-hand pane.

Question 6	*What subheadings are available in the System Stability Report section?*

17. Close Server Manager. Log off of the W2K8*zz* computer.

Exercise 6.2.2	**Using the Windows Event Viewer**
Overview	You have finished testing multiple servers to act as infrastructure servers within your organization. You will now test the Windows Event Viewer functionality within Windows Server 2008.
Outcomes	After completing this exercise, you will know how to: ▲ Launch the Windows Event Viewer ▲ Create a Custom Event Log view
Completion time	25 minutes
Precautions	If students are working in pairs, this exercise should be performed on both the odd-numbered W2K8*xx* computer and the even-numbered W2K8*yy* computer. If students are working alone, this exercise can be performed on the odd-numbered W2K8*xx* computer only.

■ PART A: WORKING WITH THE WINDOWS EVENT VIEWER

1. Log on to the W2K8*zz* computer. Click the Start button, followed by Server Manager.
2. Drill down to Diagnostics→Windows Event Viewer.

3. Expand Windows Logs.

> **Question 7**
>
> *What logs are available by default?*

4. Click Application in the left pane.

> **Question 8**
>
> *What is the most recent Event ID logged to the Application log?*

5. Click Security in the left pane.

> **Question 9**
>
> *What is the most recent Event ID logged to the Security log?*

6. Click Setup in the left pane.

> **Question 10**
>
> *What is the most recent Event ID logged to the Setup log?*

7. Click System in the left pane.

> **Question 11**
>
> *What is the most recent Event ID logged to the System log?*

■ PART B: CREATING A CUSTOM EVENT VIEWER VIEW

1. In the left-hand pane, drill down to Diagnostics→Event Viewer→Custom Views.

2. Right-click Custom Views, and click Create Custom View…. The Create Custom View screen appears.

3. In the Event level: section, place a checkmark next to Critical and Warning.

4. In the Event logs: drop-down box, expand Windows Logs, and then place a checkmark next to Application and System.

5. Click OK. The Save Filter to Custom View screen appears.

6. In the Name field, enter **Critical and Warning Events Only**. Click OK.

Question 12	How many events are displayed in this Custom View? _JI_

7. Close Server Manager. Log off of the W2K8*zz* computer.

Exercise 6.2.3	Installing and Using the Windows Network Monitor
Overview	You have finished testing multiple servers to act as infrastructure servers within your organization. You will now test Windows Network Monitor to allow you to monitor and troubleshoot network traffic in Windows Server 2008.
Outcomes	After completing this exercise, you will know how to: ▲ Install and configure Windows Network Monitor ▲ Perform a network capture ▲ Create a Capture Filter
Completion time	30 minutes
Precautions	This exercise will be completed using both the even- and odd-numbered computers. The required installers will be available from a shared folder on the \\INSTRUCTOR01\ computer, or they can be downloaded from the Microsoft Web site.

■ PART A: INSTALLING NETWORK MONITOR

1. Press Ctrl+Alt+Delete on the W2K8*zz* computer assigned to you, and log on as the default administrator of the local computer. Your username will be Administrator. The password will be MSPress#1 or the password that your instructor or lab proctor assigns to you.

2. Copy the installation file for Network Monitor from the \\INSTRUCTOR01\ computer to the root of the C:\ drive on W2K8*zz*. Double-click the file, and then click Run.

3. The Welcome to the Microsoft Network Monitor 3.1 Setup Wizard screen appears. Click Next.

4. The End-User License Agreement screen appears. Select the I accept the terms in the License Agreement radio button. Click Next.

5. The Use Microsoft Update to Help Keep your Computer Secure and Up to Date screen appears. Click the Use Microsoft Update when I check for updates (recommended) radio button. Click Next.

6. The Customer Experience Improvement Program screen appears. Select the I do not want to participate in the program at this time radio button. Click Next.

7. The Choose Setup Type screen appears. Click Complete.

8. The Ready to Install screen appears. Click Install.

NOTE	*If your lab environment does not allow Internet access, you may receive an error message about Microsoft Update. Click OK to continue if this happens.*

9. Click Finish when the installation completes.

■ PART B: USING NETWORK MONITOR TO VIEW NETWORK TRAFFIC

1. Double-click the Network Monitor 3.1 shortcut that now appears on the W2K8*zz* desktop. If this is the first time you've opened Network Monitor 3.1, the Microsoft Update Opt-In screen will appear. Click No.

2. The Microsoft Network Monitor 3.1 screen appears. Place a checkmark next to Enable conversations (consumes more memory). Click Create a new capture tab....

3. Click Capture→Start to begin a network capture. To simulate network traffic, open a command prompt, and perform an nslookup of the W2K8*xx* and W2K8*yy* computers. Close the command prompt window.

Question 13	*What is the keyboard shortcut to begin a network capture?*

4. After the capture runs for a minute, click Capture→Stop to stop the network capture.

5. In the Network Conversations pane, double-click My Traffic, and then double-click IPv4.

■ PART C: CREATING A CAPTURE FILTER

1. Click File→New→Capture. Click Filter→Capture Filter→Load Filter→Standard Filters→DNS.

Question 14	What appears in the Capture Filter pane?

2. Click Apply in the Capture Filter pane.

3. Press F10 to begin a new capture.

Question 15	Does anything appear in the Network Conversations pane? Why or why not?

4. Open a command prompt window. Key **nslookup <Name of your partner's computer>**, and press Enter.

Question 16	Does anything appear in the Network Conversations pane? Why or why not?

5. Close Network Monitor. Log off of the W2K8zz computer.

Exercise 6.2.4	Installing and Configuring WSUS
Overview	You have finished testing multiple servers to act as infrastructure servers within your organization. You now want to test Windows Server Update Services as a means of providing automated security updates to these servers.
Outcomes	After completing this exercise, you will know how to: ▲ Install and configure Windows Server Update Services ▲ Administer Windows Server Update Services ▲ Configure Windows Server Update Services client settings
Completion time	45 minutes
Precautions	Part A and B of this exercise will be completed from the odd-numbered computer. The required installers will be available on the \\INSTRUCTOR01 computer, or else they can be downloaded from the Microsoft Web site. If the lab computers do not have Internet access, the lab instructor or proctor will provide alternate configuration instructions to configure the WSUS server in Part C. If the lab computers require a proxy server to access the Internet, the lab instructor or proctor will provide the necessary configuration instructions in Part C.

■ PART A: INSTALLING WSUS PREREQUISITES ON THE ODD-NUMBERED COMPUTER

1. Press Ctrl+Alt+Delete on the W2K8*xx* computer assigned to you, and log on as the default administrator of the local computer. Your username will be Administrator. The password will be MSPress#1 or the password that your instructor or lab proctor assigns to you.

2. If the Server Manager screen does not appear automatically, click Start→Server Manager.

3. Click Roles→Add Roles. The Before You Begin screen begins. Click Next.

4. The Select Server Roles screen appears. Place a checkmark next to Web Server (IIS). (If prompted, click Add Required Role Services.)

5. Click Next twice. The Select Role Services screen appears. Place a checkmark next to the following optional components (again, if prompted, click Add Required Role Services):

   - ASP.NET

   - Windows Authentication

   - IIS 6 Management Compatibility

6. Click Next, followed by Install.

7. Click Close when the installation completes.

8. Copy the Microsoft Report Viewer installer from the \\INSTRUCTOR01\ computer to the root of the C:\ drive.

9. Open the C:\ drive in Windows Explorer. Double-click the Microsoft Report Viewer installer. Click Run to open the file.

10. The Welcome to Microsoft Report Viewer Redistributable 2005 Setup screen appears. Click Next.

11. The End-User License Agreement screen appears. Place a checkmark next to I accept the terms of the License Agreement, and click Install. Click Finish when the installation completes.

12. Log off of the W2K8*xx* computer.

■ PART B: INSTALLING WSUS 3.0 SERVICE PACK 1 ON THE ODD-NUMBERED COMPUTER

1. Press Ctrl+Alt+Delete on the W2K8*xx* computer assigned to you, and log on as the default administrator of the local computer. Your username will be Administrator. The password will be MSPress#1 or the password that your instructor or lab proctor assigns to you.

2. Copy the WSUS 3.0 SP1 installer from the \\INSTRUCTOR01\shared folder to the root of the C:\ drive.

3. Double-click the WSUS 3.0 SP1 installer. If prompted, click Run to open the file.

4. Click Next. The Installation Mode Selection screen appears. Ensure that the Full server installation including Administration Console radio button is selected, and click Next.

5. The License Agreement screen appears. Select the I Accept the terms of the License Agreement radio button, and click Next.

6. The Select Update Source screen appears. Accept the default value, and click Next.

Question 17	Where will WSUS downloads be stored by default?

7. The Database Options screen appears. Accept the default selection, and click Next.

Question 18	What database does WSUS use by default?

8. The Web Site Selection screen appears. Accept the default selection, and click Next.

9. Click Next to begin. The installation will take several minutes to complete. Click Finish when prompted.

10. Remain logged on to the W2K8*xx* computer to perform the next section.

■ PART C: PERFORMING THE INITIAL CONFIGURATION OF WSUS

1. After a short pause, the Windows Server Update Services Configuration Wizard appears. On the Before you Begin screen, click Next.

2. The Join the Microsoft Update Improvement Program screen appears. Remove the checkmark next to Yes, I would like to join the Microsoft Update Improvement Program, and then click Next.

3. The Choose Upstream Server screen appears. Ensure that the Synchronize from Microsoft Update radio button is selected, and click Next.

NOTE	*If your lab environment does not have Internet access, your lab instructor or proctor will instruct you to select the Synchronize from another Windows Server Update Services server radio button and will provide the necessary configuration information.*

4. The Specify Proxy Server screen appears. Accept the default selections, and click Next.

> **NOTE**
> *If your lab environment requires proxy server configuration, your lab instructor or proctor will instruct you to place a checkmark next to Use a proxy server when synchronizing and will provide the necessary configuration information.*

5. The Connect to Upstream Server screen appears. Click Start Connecting.

> **NOTE**
> *Establishing a connection to the Windows Update site may take several minutes before the next screen appears.*

6. Click Next. The Choose Languages screen appears. Accept the default selection, and click Next.

> **NOTE**
> *If appropriate, remove the checkmark next to English, and select the language(s) applicable to your lab environment.*

7. The Choose Products screen appears. To save disk space on the lab computers, remove the checkmark next to Office and Windows. Place a checkmark next to Windows Server 2008 and Windows Vista.

8. Click Next. The Choose Classifications screen appears. Accept the default selections, and click Next.

> **Question 19**
> *What types of udpates does WSUS download by default?*

9. Click Next. The Set Sync Schedule screen appears. Ensure that the Synchronize manually radio button is selected, and then click Next.

10. The Finished screen appears. Remove the checkmark next to Begin initial synchronization, and click Next.

11. The What's Next screen appears. Click Finish to exit the wizard.

12. Remain logged on to the W2K8*xx* computer for the next section.

■ PART D: ADMINISTERING A WSUS SERVER

1. If the Update Services MMC does not appear automatically, click Start→Administrative Tools→Microsoft Windows Server Update Services 3.0 SP1. Expand the W2K8*xx* node.

Question 20	What nodes are available under the W2K8xx node?

2. Click Synchronizations. Right-click Synchronizations, and click Synchronize Now. In the main MMC panel, the status of the Synchronization will change from Running… to Succeeded.

3. When the synchronization completes, click Options. Click Products and Classifications.

4. In the Products tab, place a checkmark next to Windows Server 2003. Click OK.

5. Log off of the W2K8*xx* computer.

■ PART E: CONFIGURING THE EVEN-NUMBERED COMPUTER TO RECEIVE UPDATES FROM WSUS

1. Log on to the W2K8*yy* computer as Administrator.

2. Open a command prompt. Confirm that you can successfully ping the W2K8*xx* computer. Close the command prompt window.

3. Click Start, key **gpedit.msc,** and click Enter.

4. The Local Group Policy Editor window appears. Browse to Computer Configuration→Administrative Templates→Windows Components→Windows Update.

5. In the right-hand pane, double-click Configure Automatic Updates.

6. The Configure Automatic Updates Properties screen appears. Select the Enabled radio button. Click OK.

7. In the right-hand pane, double-click Specify intranet Microsoft update service location.

8. The Specify Intranet Microsoft Update Service Location Properties window appears. Select Enabled. In the Set the intranet update service for detecting updates text box, enter **http://w2k8xx**. In the Set the intranet statistics server text box, enter **http://W2K8xx**. Click OK.

9. Click Start→Administrative Tools→Services. Right-click Windows Update, and click Restart.

10. Open a command prompt. At the command prompt, key **wuauclt/detectnow**, and press Enter. Close the command prompt window.

11. Log off of the W2K8*yy* computer.

■ PART F: CONFIRMING THE CONFIGURATION OF THE AUTOMATIC UPDATES CLIENT ON THE EVEN-NUMBERED COMPUTER

1. Log on to the W2K8*xx* computer as the local administrator.

2. Click Start→Administrative Tools→Update Services.

3. Expand W2K8*xx*→Computers→All Computers.

4. In the Status: drop-down box, select Any. Click Refresh.

Question 21	*What is the last status reported from the W2K8yy computer?*

5. Log off of the W2K8*xx* computer.

LAB REVIEW QUESTIONS

Completion time   15 minutes

1. In your own words, describe what you learned by completing this lab.

2. What are the IIS prerequisites needed to install WSUS 3.0 SP1?

3. What reports are available in the Update Services MMC?

4. What exception must be configured in the Windows Firewall to view Event Viewer on a remote computer?

LAB CHALLENGE: CREATING A COMPUTER GROUP IN WSUS

Completion time 30 minutes

Once you have completed testing of WSUS, you want to configure the ability to specify different lists of approved updates for different groups of computers on the Lucerne Publishing network.

After completing this exercise, you will know how to:

▲ Create a computer group in WSUS

▲ Configure a Windows Vista computer for WSUS

Precautions: If you do not complete the Lab Challenge exercises, you must still complete the Lab Cleanup steps prior to continuing on to Lab 7.1.

Create a computer group in the Update Services MMC called AllVista. Configure the VISTA*xx* computer to use W2K8*xx* for updates, and configure it to be a part of the AllVista targeted group.

LAB CLEANUP

Completion time 15 minutes

You have completed testing of Windows updating and monitoring functions and now need to reset your Windows Server 2008 computers to their original state prior to performing testing of additional infrastructure services that you are planning to deploy to your production network.

After completing this exercise, you will know how to:

▲ Remove the IIS Server role

▲ Uninstall software from a Windows Server 2008 computer

▲ Remove Local Group Policy Object configuration items

■ PART A: UNINSTALLING SOFTWARE FROM THE W2K8*ZZ* COMPUTER

1. Log on to the W2K8*zz* computer as the local administrator.

2. Click Start→Control Panel.

3. Double-click Programs and Features.

4. The Programs and Features window appears. Right-click Microsoft Network Monitor, and click Uninstall/Change.

5. Follow the prompts to uninstall the Microsoft Network Monitor.

6. Delete all installation files that you copied to the W2K8*zz* computer from the INSTRUCTOR01 computer.

7. Remove the INSTRUCTOR01 server as the W2K8*zz* computer's preferred DNS server.

8. Log off of the W2K8*zz* computer.

■ PART B: UNINSTALLING REMAINING SOFTWARE FROM THE W2K8*XX* COMPUTER

1. Log on to the W2K8*xx* computer as the local administrator.

2. Click Start→Control Panel.

3. Double-click Programs and Features.

4. The Programs and Features window appears. Right-click Microsoft Report Viewer Redistributable 2005, and click Uninstall/Change.

5. Follow the prompts to uninstall the Microsoft Report Viewer Redistributable 2005.

6. Right-click Microsoft Windows Server Update Services 3.0 SP1, and click Uninstall/Change.

7. Follow the prompts to uninstall all components of Microsoft Windows Server Update Services 3.0 SP1.

8. Click Start→Server Manager. Click Features, and then click Remove Features. Follow the prompts to uninstall the following features:

    -   Windows Internal Database

    -   Windows Process Activation Database (when prompted, click Remove Dependent Role Services)

9. Restart the computer when prompted.

10. After the server restarts, log on as the local administrator. Return to the Server Manager console. Click Roles, and then click Remove Roles. Follow the prompts to uninstall the Web Server (IIS) role.

11. Restart the computer when prompted.

■ PART C: REMOVING WSUS CONFIGURATION ON W2K8*YY*

1. Log on to the W2K8*yy* computer as the local administrator. Click Start, then key **gpedit.msc**, and click Enter.

2. Browse to Computer Configuration→Administrative Templates→Windows Components→Windows Update.

3. In the right-hand pane, double-click Configure Automatic Updates.

4. The Configure Automatic Updates Properties screen appears. Select the Not Configured radio button. Click OK.

5. In the right-hand pane, double-click Specify intranet Microsoft update service location.

6. The Specify Intranet Microsoft Update Service Location Properties window appears. Select the Not Configured radio button. Click OK.

7. Log off of the W2K8*yy* computer.

LAB 7.1
WORKING WITH DISKS

This lab contains the following exercises and activities:

BEFORE YOU BEGIN

The classroom network consists of Windows Server 2008 student servers that are all connected to a local area network. There is also a classroom server, named ServerDC, that is connected to the same classroom network. ServerDC is also running Windows Server 2008 and is the domain controller for a domain named contoso.com. Throughout the labs in this manual, you will be working with the same student server on which you will install, configure, maintain, and troubleshoot application roles, features, and services.

Your instructor should have supplied you with the information needed to fill in the following table:

Student computer name (Server##)	
Student account name (Student##)	

Working with Lab Worksheets

Each lab in this manual requires that you answer questions, shoot screen shots, or perform other activities that you are to document in a worksheet named for the lab, such as lab01_worksheet. Your instructor will supply you with the worksheet files by copying them to the Students\Worksheets share on ServerDC. As you perform the exercises in each lab, open the appropriate worksheet file using WordPad, fill in the required information, and save the file to your computer's Student##\Documents folder. This folder is automatically redirected to the ServerDC computer. Your instructor will examine these worksheet files to assess your performance.

The procedure for opening and saving a worksheet file is as follows:

1. Click Start, and then click Run. The Run dialog box appears.

2. In the Open text box, key **\\ServerDC\Students\Worksheets\lab##_worksheet** (where lab## contains the number of the lab you're completing), and click OK.

3. The worksheet document opens in Wordpad.

4. Complete all of the exercises in the worksheet.

5. In WordPad, choose Save As from the File menu. The Save As dialog box appears.

6. In the File Name text box, key **lab##_worksheet_*yourname*** (where lab## contains the number of the lab you're completing and *yourname* is your last name), and click Save.

SCENARIO

You are a server administrator working in a medium-sized organization. One morning, Karen, the manager of the Accounting department, calls to complain that she created an important document file yesterday and saved it to her departmental server, and now she can't find it. Karen goes on to explain that this sort of thing happens to her all the time; she creates files and saves them, and when she tries to open them again later, she has to spend half an hour looking for them. Sometimes she finds the file she needs, and sometimes she doesn't and is forced to create it all over again.

Because of the sensitivity of the data stored there, Karen insists on managing the Accounting server herself. When she allows you to examine the server drives, you find document files strewn about in folders everywhere, some intermixed with application files and others stored in the volume root. You decide to show Karen the basics of file management, starting with creating a new volume for the department's data files to keep them separate from the application and operating system files.

After completing this lab, you will be able to:

- Use the Disk Management snap-in to create and manage storage volumes

- Use the Diskpart.exe utility to create storage volumes

Estimated lab time: 110 minutes

Exercise 7.1.1	Creating a Simple Volume
Overview	Thanks to your instruction, Karen now sees the advantage of storing the department's data files on a volume separate from the operating system and application files. In this exercise, you create a new simple volume on the server where the accountants can store their data.
Completion time	10 minutes

1. Turn on your computer. When the logon screen appears, log on using your Student## account and the password *P@ssw0rd*.

2. Close the Initial Configuration Tasks window when it appears.

3. Click Start, and then click Administrative Tools > Computer Management. Click Continue in the User Account Control message box, and the Computer Management console appears.

4. In the scope (left) pane, click Disk Management. The Disk Management snap-in appears in the detail (right) pane, as shown in Figure 7-1-1.

5. Based on the information in the Disk Management snap-in, fill out the information in Table 7-1-1 on your lab worksheet.

Table 7-1-1
Disk Information

	Disk 0	Disk 1
Disk type (basic or dynamic)		
Total disk size		
Number and type of partitions		
Amount of unallocated space		

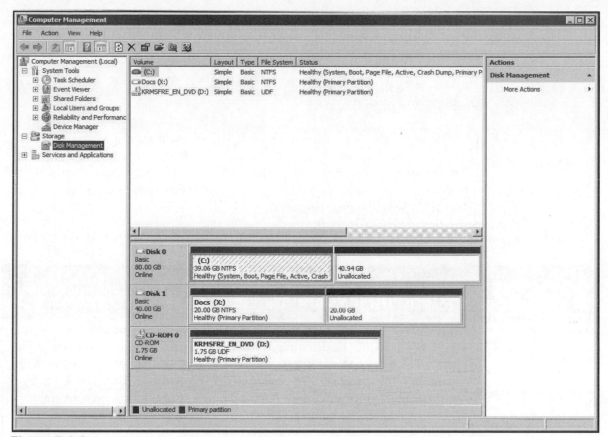

Figure 7-1-1
Disk Management snap-in

> **NOTE**
>
> *If there is not at least a gigabyte of unallocated space available on each of your computer's hard disks, see your instructor before you continue. You might have to shrink your volumes by using the Disk Management snap-in before you can proceed.*

6. In the graphical display in the bottom pane, right-click the Unallocated area of Disk 0 and, from the context menu, select New Simple Volume. The New Simple Volume Wizard appears.

7. Click Next to bypass the Welcome page. The *Specify Volume Size* page appears.

8. In the Simple volume size in MB text box, key **1000**, and click Next. The *Assign Drive Letter or Path* page appears.

9. Leave the Assign the following drive letter option selected. Choose drive letter S from the drop-down list, and then click Next. The *Format Partition* page appears.

10. Leave the Format this volume with the following settings option selected, and configure the next three parameters as follows:

- File System: NTFS
- Allocation Unit Size: Default
- Volume Label: **Karen1**

11. Select the Perform a quick format checkbox, and click Next. The *Completing the New Simple Volume Wizard* page appears.

12. Click Finish. The new volume appears in the Disk Management snap-in.

13. Press Ctrl+Prt Scr to take a screen shot of the Disk Management snap-in, showing the volume you created, and then press Ctrl+V to paste the resulting image into the lab07_1_worksheet file in the page provided.

14. Leave the Computer Management console open for future exercises.

Exercise 7.1.2	Extending a Volume
Overview	A few days later, you receive another call from Karen. She has been diligently moving the department's data files to the volume you created for her, but she has now run out of disk space. The volume was not big enough! To address the problem, you decide to extend the Karen1 volume by using some of the unallocated space left on the disk. For this task, you intend to use the Diskpart.exe command line utility.
Completion time	15 minutes

1. Click Start, and then click All Programs > Accessories > Windows Explorer.

2. In the folders pane, expand the Computer container, and locate the S: drive you created in Exercise 7-1-1.

3. Right-click the S: drive and, from the context menu, select New > Folder. Give the new folder the name **WinSvr2008**.

4. Click Start, and then click Run. The Run dialog box appears.

5. In the Open text box, key **\\serverdc\install\WinSvr2008**, and click OK. A second Explorer window appears, displaying the contents of the WinSvr2008 folder on the classroom server, as shown in Figure 7-1-2.

6. Select the entire contents of the WinSvr2008 folder on ServerDC, and drag it to the S:\WinSvr2008 folder you created on your computer.

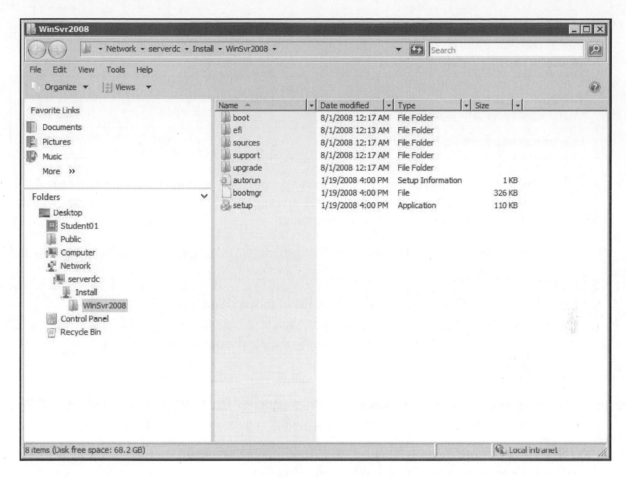

Figure 7-1-2
WinSvr2008 folder on ServerDC

| Question 1 | *What is the result?* |

7. Click Cancel.

8. Consult the Disk Management snap-in, and fill out Table 7-1-2 with the amount of unallocated space left on the drives in gigabytes and megabytes.

> NOTE
>
> *The best way to determine the amount of space is to right-click on each unallocated space, select Properties, and then select the Volumes tab.*

Table 7-1-2
Unallocated Space Remaining

	Disk 0	Disk 1
Unallocated space left (gigabytes)		
Unallocated space left (megabytes)		

9. Open the Run dialog box. In the Open text box, key **diskpart**, and press Enter. Click Continue in the User Account Control message box, and a Command Prompt window appears containing the DISKPART > prompt.

10. Key **select disk 0**, and press Enter. The program responds, saying that Disk 0 is now the selected disk.

11. Key **list partition**, and press Enter. A list of the partitions on Disk 0 appears.

Question 2	*What is the number of the 1-GB partition you created earlier in this exercise?*

12. Key **select partition #**, where # is the number of the 1-GB partition, and press Enter. The program responds, saying that Partition # is now the selected partition.

13. Key **extend size =** *xxxx*, where *xxxx* is the amount of unallocated space left on the drive, in megabytes, from Table 7-1-2. Then, press Enter.

Question 3	*What is the result?*

14. Press Ctrl+Prt Scr to take a screen shot of the Disk Management snap-in, showing the extended volume, and then press Ctrl+V to paste the resulting image into the lab07_1_worksheet file in the page provided.

15. In the Diskpart window, key **exit**, and press Enter to terminate the Diskpart program.

16. Try again to copy the entire contents of the WinSvr2008 folder on ServerDC to the S:\WinSvr2008 folder on your computer.

Question 4	*What is the result?*

17. Leave the Disk Management snap-in open for the next exercise.

Exercise 7.1.3	Creating Additional Volumes
Overview	Karen is thrilled at the idea of storing her department's data files in separate volumes, and now she wants you to create more partitions on her server. However, you used all of the available space to create her Karen1 volume. Therefore, you have to shrink the Karen1 volume to create room for the additional volumes she wants.
Completion time	10 minutes

1. In the Disk Management snap-in, right-click the Karen1 volume you created on Disk 0 and, from the context menu, select Shrink Volume. The Shrink S: dialog box appears, as shown in Figure 7-1-3.

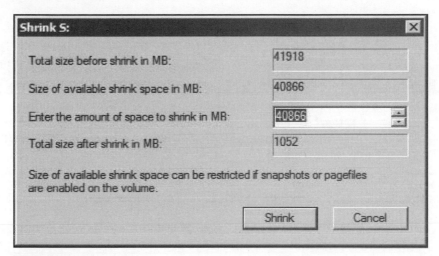

Figure 7-1-3
Shrink S: dialog box

Question 5	How much available shrink space is contained in the volume?

2. In the Enter the amount of space to shrink in MB spin box, key the amount of available shrink space minus 2000 MB (2 GB).

3. Click Shrink. The amount of space you entered appears as unallocated space in the Disk Management snap-in.

4. Right-click the unallocated space in Disk 0, and select New Simple Volume. The New Simple Volume Wizard appears.

5. Use the wizard to create a new 2000-MB partition, using the drive letter T, the NTFS file system, the volume name **Karen2**, and the Quick Format option.

6. Repeat steps 4 and 5 to create another 2000-MB partition, using the drive letter U, the NTFS file system, and the volume name **Karen3**.

Question 6	How is the last volume you created different from the previous ones? Explain why.

Question 7	What do you suppose would happen if you created another simple volume out of the free space left on the disk?

7. Press Ctrl+Prt Scr to take a screen shot of the Disk Management snap-in, showing the volumes you created, and then press Ctrl+V to paste the resulting image into the lab07_1_worksheet file in the page provided.

8. Leave the Computer Management console open for the next exercise.

Exercise 7.1.4	Mounting a Volume
Overview	Karen calls yet again to tell you that she needs still more space on her Karen1 volume, but is unable to expand it. You decide to provide her with additional space by creating a volume and mounting it in a folder on the Karen1 volume.
Completion time	15 minutes

1. In the Disk Management snap-in, right-click the Karen1 volume you created in Exercise 7.1.1, and try to extend it by 2000 MB.

Question 8	Were you successful?

2. Right-click the Karen3 volume you created in Exercise 7.1.3 and, from the context menu, select Extend Volume. The Extend Volume Wizard appears.

3. Click Next to bypass the Welcome page. The *Select Disks* page appears, as shown in Figure 7-1-4.

4. In the Select the amount of space in MB spin box, key **2000**, and click Next. The *Completing the Extend Volume Wizard* page appears.

5. Click Finish.

Question 9	*What is the result?*

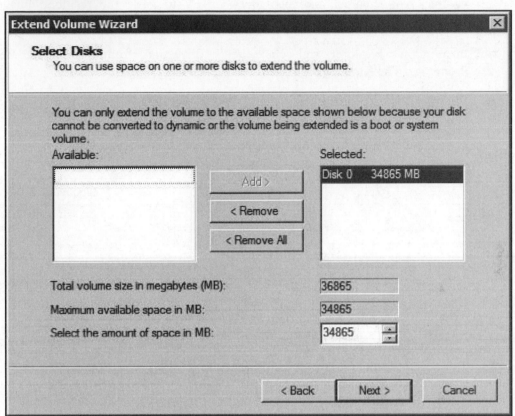

Figure 7-1-4
Select Disks page of the Extend Volume Wizard

6. Open Windows Explorer, and create a new folder on the computer's S: drive named **Karen4**.

7. In the Disk Management snap-in, right-click the remaining Free Space element on Disk 0 and, from the context menu, select New Simple Volume. The New Simple Volume Wizard appears.

8. On the *Specify Volume Size* page, specify a volume size of **2000** MB, and then click Next.

9. On the *Assign Drive Letter or Path* page, select the Mount in the following empty NTFS folder option. In the text box, key **S:\Karen4**, and click Next.

10. On the *Format Partition* page, select the NTFS file system and, in the Volume label text box, key **Karen4**.

11. Select the Perform a quick format checkbox, and click Next.

12. Click Finish to create the volume.

13. Press Ctrl+Prt Scr to take a screen shot of the Disk Management snap-in, showing the volumes you created, and then press Ctrl+V to paste the resulting image into the lab07_1_worksheet file in the page provided.

14. In Windows Explorer, right-click the S: drive and, from the context menu, select Properties. The Karen1 (S:) Properties sheet appears.

15. Fill out Table 7-1-3 with the amount of used, free, and total space on the S: drive in gigabytes and megabytes.

Table 7-1-3
Karen1 (S:) Properties

	Megabytes	**Gigabytes**
Used space		
Free space		
Capacity		

Question 10	Does the capacity of the S: drive reflect the addition of the mounted Karen4 volume?

16. Click OK to close the Karen1 (S:) Properties sheet.

17. Select the S:\Karen4 icon.

NOTE	If the status bar does not appear at the bottom of the Windows Explorer window, activate it by selecting Status Bar from the View menu.

Question 11	According to the status bar, how much free space is on the Karen4 volume?

Question 12	Does the free space on Karen4 reflect the space available on the Karen1 volume as well?

18. Close all Windows Explorer windows.

19. Leave the Computer Management console open for the next exercise.

Exercise 7.1.5	Removing Volumes
Overview	The Accounting department server currently has five volumes on its disk: three primary partitions and one extended partition with two logical drives. Karen and her staff have found it difficult to manage their files with so many volumes, so she wants to consolidate the disk into just two volumes: her original volume, plus one large data volume, which will be a spanned volume that uses all of the available space on Disk 0 plus all of the space on the second hard disk in the computer.
Completion time	10 minutes

1. In the Disk Management snap-in, right-click the Karen4 volume and, from the context menu, select Delete Volume. A Delete Simple Volume message box appears, warning you that deleting the volume will erase all of the data stored on it.

2. Click Yes. The volume is deleted.

3. Repeat steps 1 and 2 to delete the Karen3 volume.

Question 13	*Why doesn't the disk space used by the Karen3 and Karen4 volumes appear in the Disk Management snap in as unallocated?*

4. Repeat steps 1 and 2 to delete the Karen2 volume.

5. Right-click the Karen1 volume and, from the context menu, select Extend Volume. The Extend Volume Wizard appears.

6. Click Next to bypass the Welcome page. The *Select Disks* page appears.

Question 14	*What is the maximum amount of space that you can use to extend the Karen1 volume?*

Question 15	*Why can't you extend the Karen1 volume by using all of the remaining space on the disk?*

7. Click Cancel to close the wizard.

8. Repeat steps 1 and 2 to delete all of the volumes on both of the computer's disks, including the extended partition on Disk 0, except for the original C: volume and the Karen1 volume you created in Exercise 7.1.1.

9. Leave the Disk Management snap-in open for the next exercise.

Exercise 7.1.6	Creating a Spanned Volume
Overview	Now that you have deleted the extra volumes on the Accounting server, you can extend the Karen1 volume to use all of the disk space on both of the computer's hard drives.
Completion time	10 minutes

1. In the Disk Management snap-in, right-click the Karen1 volume and, from the context menu, select Extend Volume. The Extend Volume Wizard appears.

2. Click Next to bypass the Welcome page. The *Select Disks* page appears.

Question 16	*What is the maximum amount of space that you can use to extend the Karen1 volume?*

Question 17	*Why can't you extend the Karen1 volume to the second hard disk (Disk 1)?*

3. Press Ctrl+Prt Scr to take a screen shot of the *Select Disks* page, and then press Ctrl+V to paste the resulting image into the lab07_1_worksheet file in the page provided.

4. Click Cancel to close the wizard.

5. Right-click the Disk 0 box and, from the context menu, select Convert to Dynamic Disk. The Convert to Dynamic Disk dialog box appears, as shown in Figure 7-1-5.

6. Select both the Disk 0 and Disk 1 checkboxes, and click OK. The Disks to Convert dialog box appears.

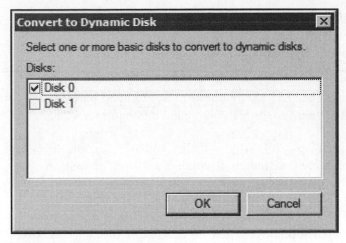

Figure 7-1-5
Convert to Dynamic Disk dialog box

7. Click Convert. A Disk Management message box appears, warning you that you cannot dual-boot a computer from a dynamic disk.

8. Click Yes. Both of the disks are converted from basic to dynamic disks.

9. Once again, right-click the Karen1 volume and, from the context menu, select Extend Volume. The Extend Volume Wizard appears.

10. Click Next to bypass the Welcome page. The *Select Disks* page appears.

Question 18	How is the Select Disks page different now that you have converted the basic disks to dynamic disks?

11. Select Disk 1 in the Available box, and click Add. Disk 1 moves to the Selected box.

Question 19	What is the total volume size displayed on the Select Disks page?

12. Click Next. The *Completing the Extend Volume Wizard* page appears.

13. Click Finish. The Karen1 volume expands to encompass all of the available space on both disks.

14. Press Ctrl+Prt Scr to take a screen shot of the Disk Management snap-in, showing the spanned volume you created, and then press Ctrl+V to paste the resulting image into the lab07_1_worksheet file in the page provided.

15. Close the Computer Management console, and log off of the computer.

LAB REVIEW QUESTIONS

Completion time	10 minutes

1. In Exercise 7.1.5, why doesn't the extended partition you created appear in the Disk Management snap-in's volume list in the top view pane?

2. In Exercise 7.1.4, why is it that you were unable to extend the Karen1 volume and were forced to mount a volume to a folder instead, but you were able to extend Karen3?

3. In Exercise 7.1.6 after you converted Disk 0 from a basic disk to a dynamic disk, how many partitions were there on the disk? How do you know?

4. If one of the hard disk drives should fail after creating the spanned volume on the Accounting server by using space from both hard disks, what would happen to the data stored on the volume?

LAB CHALLENGE: CREATING A STRIPED VOLUME

Completion time	20 minutes

Karen wants to increase the disk performance on her server and has decided that, instead of a single spanned volume, she wants to create a single striped volume as large as her server can support. To complete this challenge, delete the Karen1 spanned volume, and re-create it as a striped volume using the same file system and formatting parameters. To complete these tasks, you can use only the Diskpart.exe utility. List the Diskpart commands you used. When you are finished, open the Disk Management snap-in, and press Ctrl+Prt Scr to take a screen shot, showing the striped volume you created. Then, press Ctrl+V to paste the resulting image into the lab07_1_worksheet file in the page provided.

WORKSTATION RESET: RETURNING TO BASELINE

Completion time	10 minutes

To return the computer to its baseline state, complete the following procedure.

1. Open the Disk Management snap-in.

2. Delete all of the volumes on both disks except for the original C: volume that contains the operating system.

LAB 8.1
MONITORING SERVERS

This lab contains the following exercises and activities:

Exercise 8.1.1   Using Event Viewer

Exercise 8.1.2   Using Performance Monitor

Exercise 8.1.3   Establishing a Baseline

Exercise 8.1.4   Viewing Data Collector Set Logs

Exercise 8.1.5   Using Reliability Monitor

Lab Review   Questions

Lab Challenge   Creating a Performance Counter Alert

BEFORE YOU BEGIN

The classroom network consists of Windows Server 2008 student servers that are all connected to a local area network. There is also a classroom server, named ServerDC, that is connected to the same classroom network. ServerDC is also running Windows Server 2008 and is the domain controller for a domain named contoso.com. Throughout the labs in this manual, you will be working with the same student server on which you will install, configure, maintain, and troubleshoot application roles, features, and services.

Your instructor should have supplied you with the information needed to fill in the following table:

Student computer name (Server##)	
Student account name (Student##)	

To complete the exercises in this lab, you will require access to a second student computer on the classroom network, referred to in the exercises as your *partner server*. Depending on the configuration of your network, use one of the following options as directed by your instructor:

- For a conventional classroom network with one operating system installed on each computer, you must have a lab partner with his or her own computer, performing the same exercises as yourself.

- For a classroom in which each computer uses local virtualization software to install multiple operating systems, you must run two virtual machines representing student computers and perform the exercises separately on each virtual machine.

- For a classroom that uses online virtualization, you will have access to two virtual student servers in your Web browser. You must perform the exercises separately on each virtual machine.

Working with Lab Worksheets

Each lab in this manual requires that you answer questions, shoot screen shots, or perform other activities that you are to document in a worksheet named for the lab, such as lab01_worksheet. Your instructor will supply you with the worksheet files by copying them to the Students\Worksheets share on ServerDC. As you perform the exercises in each lab, open the appropriate worksheet file using WordPad, fill in the required information, and save the file to your computer's Student##\Documents folder. This folder is automatically redirected to the ServerDC computer. Your instructor will examine these worksheet files to assess your performance.

The procedure for opening and saving a worksheet file is as follows:

1. Click Start, and then click Run. The Run dialog box appears.

2. In the Open text box, key **\\ServerDC\Students\Worksheets\lab##_worksheet** (where lab## contains the number of the lab you're completing), and click OK.

3. The worksheet document opens in WordPad.

4. Complete all of the exercises in the worksheet.

5. In WordPad, choose Save As from the File menu. The Save As dialog box appears.

6. In the File Name text box, key **lab##_worksheet_*yourname*** (where lab## contains the number of the lab you're completing and *yourname* is your last name), and click Save.

SCENARIO

Your assignment today in your company's network test lab is to introduce your group of new hires to basic server monitoring procedures. To do this, you are going to demonstrate how to use tools such as the Event Viewer console, the Performance Monitor snap-in, and data collector sets.

After completing this lab, you will be able to:

- Create filters and custom views in the Event Viewer console

- Monitor system performance and reliability using the Reliability and Performance Monitor console

Estimated lab time: 100 minutes

Exercise 8.1.1	Using Event Viewer
Overview	In this exercise, you demonstrate some methods for isolating the most important events in the Windows Server 2008 logs.
Completion time	10 minutes

1. Turn on your computer. When the logon screen appears, log on to the domain with your Student## account, where ## is the number assigned by your instructor, using the password *P@ssw0rd*.

2. Click Start, and then click Administrative Tools > Event Viewer. Click Continue in the User Account Control message box, and the Event Viewer console appears, as shown in Figure 8-1-1.

3. Expand the Windows Logs folder, and select the System log. The contents of the log appear in the detail pane.

> **Question 1** *How many events appear in the System log?.*

4. In the actions pane, click Filter Current Log. The Filter Current Log dialog box appears.

5. In the Event Level area, select the Critical and Warning checkboxes, and then click OK.

> **Question 2** *How many events appear in the System log now?*

6. In the actions pane, click Create Custom View. The Create Custom View dialog box appears.

7. In the Logged drop-down list, select Last 7 days.

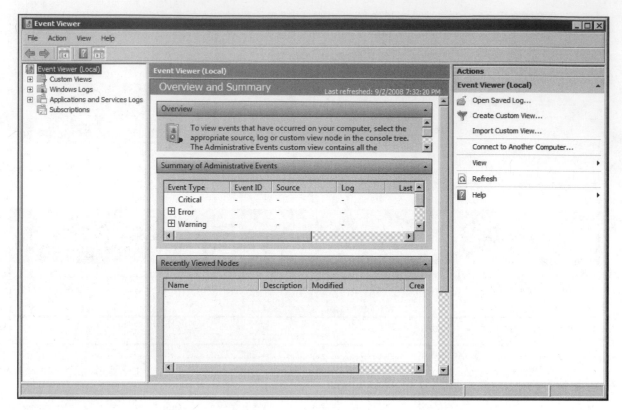

Figure 8-1-1
Event Viewer console

8. In the Event Level area, select the Critical and Warning checkboxes.

9. Leave the By log option selected and, in the Event logs drop-down list, select the Application, Security, and System checkboxes under Windows Logs.

10. Click OK. The Save Filter to Custom View dialog box appears.

11. In the Name text box, key **Critical & Warning**, and then click OK. The Critical & Warning view appears in the Custom Views folder.

Question 3	*How many events appear in the Critical & Warning custom view?*

12. Press Ctrl+Prt Scr to take a screen shot of the Event Viewer console, showing the Critical & Warning custom view, and then press Ctrl+V to paste the resulting image into the lab08_1_worksheet file in the page provided.

13. Close the Event Viewer console.

14. Leave the computer logged on for the next exercise.

Exercise 8.1.2	Using Performance Monitor
Overview	In this exercise, you demonstrate the company's performance-monitoring policies by configuring a graph in the Performance Monitor snap-in.
Completion time	15 minutes

1. Click Start, and then click Administrative Tools > Reliability and Performance Monitor. Click Continue in the User Account Control message box, and the Reliability and Performance Monitor console appears.

2. Select the Performance Monitor node. The default Performance Monitor graph appears, as shown in Figure 8-1-2.

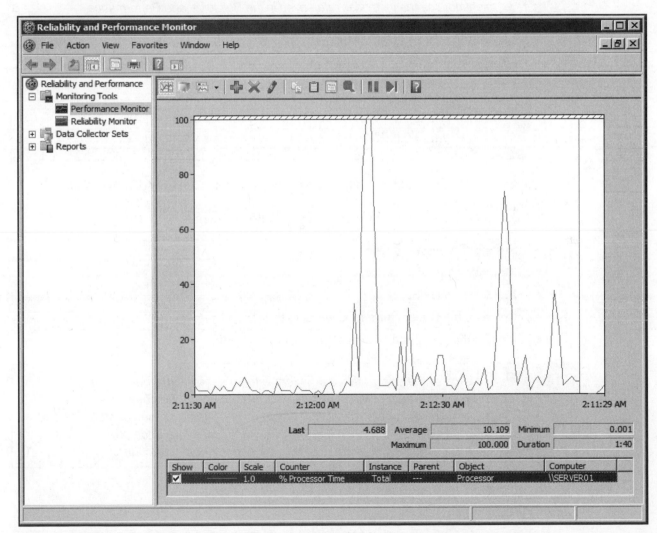

Figure 8-1-2
Performance Monitor snap-in

Question 4	What counter appears in the Performance Monitor display by default?

3. Click the Add button in the toolbar. The Add Counters dialog box appears.

4. In the Available counters list, expand the Server Work Queues entry.

5. Select the Queue Length counter.

6. In the Instances of selected object list, select 0, and then click Add. The Queue Length counter appears in the Added counters list.

NOTE	Depending on the configuration of your classroom computers, you might or might not see the instances referenced in the Reliability and Performance Monitor exercises. If no instances appear, you can proceed to add the selected performance counters without affecting the outcome of the exercise.

7. Click OK to close the Add Counters dialog box.

Question 5	What happens?

8. Click the Add button in the toolbar once again. The Add Counters dialog box appears.

9. Repeat steps 4 to 6 to select the following additional counters:

- System: Processor Queue Length
- Memory: Page Faults/Sec
- Memory: Pages/Sec
- Network Interface: Output Queue Length
- PhysicalDisk (_Total): Current Disk Queue Length

NOTE	For each of the performance counters listed, the first term (before the colon) is the name of the performance object in which the counter is located. The second term (after the colon) is the name of the counter itself. A value in parentheses appearing after the performance object name (immediately before the colon) is the instance of the counter.

10. Click OK to close the Add Counters dialog box.

Question 6	Does this selection of counters make for an effective graph? Why or why not?

11. Minimize the Reliability and Performance Monitor console, and launch any three new programs from the Start menu.

12. Restore the Reliability and Performance Monitor console.

Question 7	What effect does launching the programs have on the Performance Monitor graph?

13. Click the Properties button on the toolbar. The Performance Monitor Properties sheet appears.

14. Click the Graph tab.

15. In the Vertical Scale box, change the value of the Maximum field to 200, and click OK.

Question 8	Does this modification make the graph easier or more difficult to read? Why or why not?

16. Press Ctrl+Prt Scr to take a screen shot of the Performance Monitor snap-in, showing the line graph, and then press Ctrl+V to paste the resulting image into the lab08_1_worksheet file in the page provided.

17. Click Window > New Window. A new Reliability and Performance Monitor window appears.

18. Display the Performance Monitor graph in the new window.

19. Click the Add button, and add the following counters to the Performance Monitor graph:

- Network Interface (All Instances): Packets/Sec
- Network Interface (All Instances): Output Queue Length
- Server: Bytes Total/Sec

20. Click OK to close the Add Counters dialog box and add the counters to the graph.

Question 9	Does this selection of counters make for an effective graph? Why or why not?

21. Leave the Reliability and Performance Monitor console open for the next exercise.

Exercise 8.1.3	Establishing a Baseline
Overview	In this exercise, you create a data collector set that will capture baseline performance levels for your computer.
Completion time	20 minutes

1. In the Reliability and Performance Monitor console, expand the Data Collector Sets folder.

2. Right-click the User Defined folder and, from the context menu, select New > Data Collector Set. The Create New Data Collector Set Wizard appears, displaying the *How would you like to create this new data collector set?* page, as shown in Figure 8-1-3.

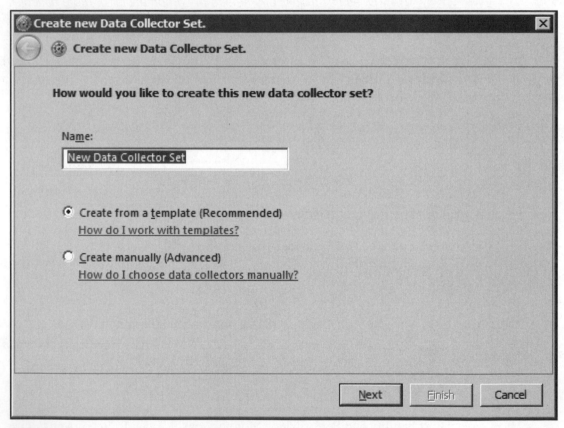

Figure 8-1-3
Create New Data Collector Set Wizard

3. In the Name text box, key **Server## Baseline**, where ## is the number assigned to your computer.

4. Select the Create manually (Advanced) option, and click Next. The *What type of data do you want to include?* page appears.

5. Select the Performance counter checkbox, and click Next. The *Which performance counters would you like to log?* page appears.

6. Click Add. The same dialog box appears that you used for adding counters in Exercise 8.1.2.

7. Add the following performance counters:

    -   LogicalDisk (All instances): % Free Space
    -   Memory: Available Mbytes
    -   Memory: Committed Bytes
    -   Memory: Page Faults/Sec
    -   Memory: Pages/Sec
    -   Memory: Pool Non-paged Bytes
    -   Network Interface (All instances): Bytes Total/sec
    -   Network Interface (All instances): Output Queue Length
    -   PhysicalDisk (All instances): % Disk Time
    -   PhysicalDisk (All instances): Avg. Disk Bytes/Transfer
    -   PhysicalDisk (All instances): Current Disk Queue Length
    -   PhysicalDisk (All instances): Disk Bytes/sec
    -   Processor (All instances): % Processor Time
    -   Processor (All instances): Interrupts/sec
    -   Server: Bytes Total/Sec
    -   Server Work Queues (All instances): Queue Length
    -   System: Processor Queue Length

8. Click OK to add the counters to the Performance counters list.

9. Press Ctrl+Prt Scr to take a screen shot of the Create New Data Collector Set Wizard, showing the performance counters you added, and then press Ctrl+V to paste the resulting image into the lab08_1_worksheet file in the page provided.

10. Set the Sample interval spin box to 5 Seconds, and click Next. The *Where would you like the data to be saved page?* appears.

11. Click Next to accept the default setting. The *Create the data collector set?* page appears.

12. Click Finish to accept the default Save and close option. The new data collector set appears in the User defined folder.

13. Right-click the Server## Baseline data collector set and, from the context menu, select Properties. The Server## Baseline Properties sheet appears.

14. Click the Stop Condition tab.

15. Select the Overall duration checkbox. Then, set the spin box value to 5 Minutes, and click OK.

16. Select the Server## Baseline data collector set, and click the Start button. The data collector set begins running.

17. Select the User Defined folder, and wait five minutes until the status of the Server## Baseline data collector set is Stopped.

18. Leave the Reliability and Performance Monitor console open for the next exercise.

Exercise 8.1.4	Viewing Data Collector Set Logs
Overview	In this exercise, you demonstrate some methods for isolating the most important events in the Windows Server 2008 logs.
Completion time	10 minutes

1. In the Reliability and Performance Monitor console, select the User Defined folder.

2. Right-click the Server## Baseline data collector set you created in Exercise 8.1.3 and, from the context menu, select Latest Report. A line graph appears, displaying the data you just collected.

3. In the legend below the graph, select the % Processor Time counter, and press Ctrl-H.

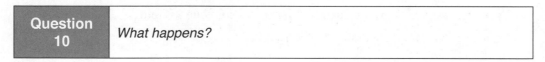

Question 10	*What happens?*

4. Press Ctrl+Prt Scr to take a screen shot of the Reliability and Performance Monitor console, showing the line graph, and then press Ctrl+V to paste the resulting image into the lab08_1_worksheet file in the page provided.

5. Press Ctrl-H again.

6. In the legend, click the Object column heading to re-sort the list.

7. In the Show column, clear all of the checkboxes except those of the Memory counters.

8. Click the Properties button on the toolbar. The Performance Monitor Properties sheet appears.

9. Click the Graph tab.

10. In the View drop-down list, select Area.

11. In the Vertical Scale box, change Maximum field to an appropriate value for the data currently displayed in the graph, and click OK.

12. Press Ctrl+Prt Scr to take another screen shot of the Reliability and Performance Monitor console, showing the revised line graph, and then press Ctrl+V paste the resulting image into the lab08_1_worksheet file in the page provided.

13. Leave the Reliability and Performance Monitor console open for the next exercise.

Exercise 8.1.5	Using Reliability Monitor
Overview	In this exercise, you demonstrate how the Reliability Monitor snap-in evaluates the computer's stability.
Completion time	15 minutes

1. In the Reliability and Performance Monitor console, select the Reliability Monitor node. The System Stability Chart and System Stability Report appear in the detail pane, as shown in Figure 8-1-4.

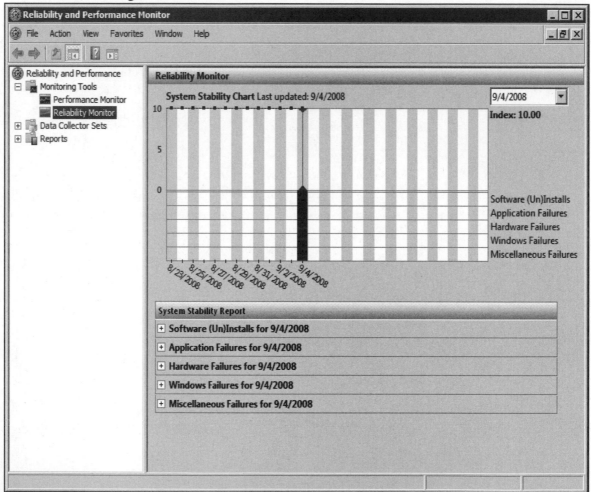

Figure 8-1-4
Reliability Monitor snap-in

Question 11	*What is your computer's current stability index?*

2. Turn the computer's power switch off without performing a proper system shutdown.

3. Wait 30 seconds, and turn the computer back on.

4. When the Windows Error Recovery menu appears, select Start Windows Normally. Windows loads, and the Shutdown Event Tracker dialog box appears.

5. In the *Why did my computer shut down unexpectedly?* drop-down list, select Power Failure: Environment, and click OK.

6. Click Start, and then click Control Panel. The Control Panel window appears.

7. Double-click Date and Time. The Date and Time dialog box appears.

8. Click Change date and time. Click Continue in the User Account Control message box, and the Date and Time Settings dialog box appears.

9. In the calendar, select tomorrow's date, and click OK.

NOTE	*Under normal conditions, the Reliability Monitor only processes entire days' worth of events at a time. For the purposes of this exercise, you will be setting the computer's calendar forward temporarily to force the program to process today's events. If you are unable to set the calendar forward, as in some virtual machine scenarios, you might have to wait until tomorrow or your next class to complete this exercise.*

10. Click OK to close the Date and Time dialog box.

11. Click Start, and then click Administrative Tools > Task Scheduler. Click Continue in the User Account Control message box, and the Task Scheduler console appears.

12. In the scope pane, expand the Task Scheduler Library, Microsoft, and Windows folders. Then, select the RAC folder.

13. Click View > Show Hidden Tasks. The RACAgent task appears in the detail pane.

14. Select the RACAgent task and, in the actions pane, click Run.

15. In the detail pane, select the History tab. Then, in the actions pane, click Refresh. Make sure that the task is completed before you continue.

16. Close the Task Scheduler console.

17. Click Start, and then click Administrative Tools > Reliability and Performance Monitor. Click Continue in the User Account Control message box, and the Reliability and Performance Monitor console appears.

18. Select the Reliability Monitor node.

19. Click the red X mark on today's date.

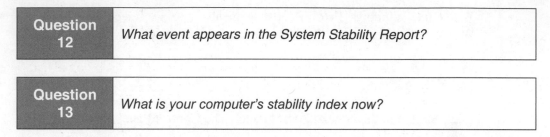

Question 12	*What event appears in the System Stability Report?*

Question 13	*What is your computer's stability index now?*

20. Press Ctrl+Prt Scr to take a screen shot of the Reliability Monitor display, and then press Ctrl+V to paste the resulting image into the lab08_1_worksheet file in the page provided.

21. Open the Date and Time dialog box again, and reset the computer to the correct date.

22. Close all open windows, and log off of the computer.

LAB REVIEW QUESTIONS

Completion time	10 minutes

1. In Exercise 8.1.1, how does the filtered view that you created first in the Event Viewer console differ from the Critical & Warning custom view you created?

2. In Exercise 8.1.2, when you added the Server Work Queues: Queue Length counter to the Performance Monitor graph, you selected the instance 0. Under what conditions would there be three additional instances numbered 1, 2, and 3?

3. In Exercise 8.1.2, how would using the report view instead of the line graph view affect the compatibility of the performance counters you select?

4. When creating a performance counter collector set, under what circumstances would it be necessary to specify a user name and password in the Run As section of the collector set's Properties sheet?

LAB CHALLENGE: CREATING A PERFORMANCE COUNTER ALERT

Completion time	20 minutes

Your supervisor is concerned that the new workstations in the test lab might not have sufficient memory, and she wants to gather information about memory consumption when the systems are operating at peak capacity. As a result, you have been instructed to log performance data for 60 minutes when the available memory on the computers drops below half of the installed memory capacity. To complete this challenge, you must use the Reliability and Performance Monitor console to create a performance counter alert that monitors the computer's available memory and starts logging when the available memory is low. List the steps you performed to create the alert.

> **NOTE**   *No workstation reset is necessary before beginning the next lab.*

LAB 9.1
BACKING UP

This lab contains the following exercises and activities:

Exercise 9.1.1	Installing Windows Server Backup
Exercise 9.1.2	Creating a Backup Volume
Exercise 9.1.3	Performing a Single Backup
Exercise 9.1.4	Running an Incremental Backup
Exercise 9.1.5	Recovering Data
Lab Review	Questions
Lab Challenge	Scheduling a Backup Job

BEFORE YOU BEGIN

The classroom network consists of Windows Server 2008 student servers that are all connected to a local area network. There is also a classroom server, named ServerDC, that is connected to the same classroom network. ServerDC is also running Windows Server 2008 and is the domain controller for a domain named contoso.com. Throughout the labs in this manual, you will be working with the same student server on which you will install, configure, maintain, and troubleshoot application roles, features, and services.

Your instructor should have supplied you with the information needed to fill in the following table:

Student computer name (Server##)	
Student account name (Student##)	

Working with Lab Worksheets

Each lab in this manual requires that you answer questions, shoot screen shots, or perform other activities that you are to document in a worksheet named for the lab, such as

204

lab01 worksheet. Your instructor will supply you with the worksheet files by copying them to the Students\Worksheets share on ServerDC. As you perform the exercises in each lab, open the appropriate worksheet file using WordPad, fill in the required information, and save the file to your computer's Student##\Documents folder. This folder is automatically redirected to the ServerDC computer. Your instructor will examine these worksheet files to assess your performance.

The procedure for opening and saving a worksheet file is as follows:

1. Click Start, and then click Run. The Run dialog box appears.

2. In the Open text box, key **\\ServerDC\Students\Worksheets\lab##_worksheet** (where lab## contains the number of the lab you're completing), and click OK.

3. The worksheet document opens in WordPad.

4. Complete all of the exercises in the worksheet.

5. In WordPad, choose Save As from the File menu. The Save As dialog box appears.

6. In the File Name text box, key **lab##_worksheet_*yourname*** (where lab## contains the number of the lab you're completing and *yourname* is your last name), and click Save.

SCENARIO

Your assignment today in your company's network test lab is to examine the capabilities of the new Windows Server Backup tool included in Windows Server 2008.

After completing this lab, you will be able to:

- Install Windows Server Backup and use it to create full and incremental backup jobs

- Restore files from a backup

- Create a scheduled backup job

Estimated lab time: 90 minutes

Exercise 9.1.1	Installing Windows Server Backup
Overview	In this exercise, you install the backup software that is included as a feature with Windows Server 2008.
Completion time	5 minutes

1. Turn on your computer. When the logon screen appears, log on to the domain with your Student## account, where ## is the number assigned by your instructor, using the password *P@ssw0rd*.

2. Click Start, and then click Administrative Tools > Server Manager. Click Continue in the User Account Control message box, and the Server Manager console appears.

3. In the scope pane, select the Features node.

4. In the detail pane, click Add Features. The Add Features Wizard appears, displaying the *Select Features* page.

5. Under Windows Server Backup Features, select the Windows Server Backup and Command-line Tools checkboxes, as shown in Figure 9-1-1. An Add features required for Command-line Tools? dialog box appears.

6. Click Add Required Features, and then click Next. The *Confirm Installation Selections* page appears.

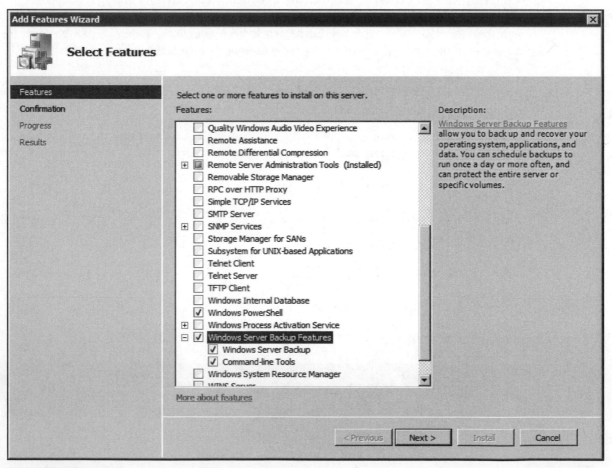

Figure 9-1-1
Windows Server Backup Features

7.   Click Install. The wizard installs the features.

8.   Click Close. The wizard closes.

9.   Close the Server Manager console.

10. Leave the computer logged on for the next exercise.

Exercise 9.1.2	Creating a Backup Volume
Overview	In this exercise, you create the volume that you will use to back up your Windows Server 2008 computer.
Completion time	15 minutes

1.   Click Start, and then click Administrative Tools > Computer Management. Click Continue in the User Account Control message box, and the Computer Management console appears.

2.   Select the Disk Management node, as shown in Figure 9-1-2.

3.   If there are any volumes on Disk 1, right-click each one and, from the context menu, select Delete Volume. A message box appears, warning you that deleting the volume will erase any data on it.

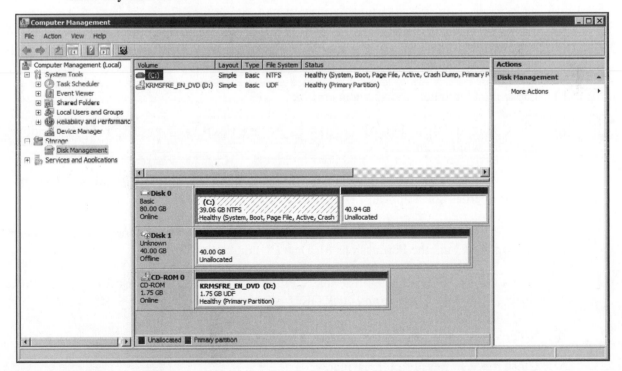

Figure 9-1-2
Disk Management snap-in

4. Click Yes. The volume is deleted.

5. When all of the space on Disk 1 is unallocated, right-click the unallocated space and, from the context menu, select New Simple Volume. The New Simple Volume Wizard appears.

6. Click Next to bypass the Welcome page. The *Specify Volume Size* page appears.

7. Click Next to use all of the available space for the volume. The *Assign Drive Letter or Path* page appears.

8. In the Assign the following drive letter drop-down list, select letter Z, and then click Next. The *Format Partition* page appears.

9. In the Volume Label text box, key **Backup**.

10. Select the Perform a quick format checkbox, and click Next. The *Completing the New Simple Volume Wizard* page appears.

11. Click Finish. The wizard creates the volume.

12. If there is no second partition on Disk 0, repeat steps 5 to 11 to create a simple volume from all of the unallocated space on the disk, using the drive letter X and the volume name **Data**.

13. Press Ctrl+Prt Scr to take a screen shot of the Computer Management console, showing the volume(s) you just created, and then press Ctrl+V to paste the resulting image into the lab09_1_worksheet file in the page provided.

14. Close the Computer Management console.

15. Click Start, and then click All Programs > Accessories > Windows Explorer. A Windows Explorer window appears.

16. Right-click the Data (X:) volume and, from the context menu, select Properties. The Data (X:) Properties sheet appears.

17. Click the Security tab, and then click Edit. Click Continue in the User Account Control message box, and the Permissions for Data (X:) dialog box appears.

18. In the Group or user names list, select Everyone. In the Permissions for Everyone list, select Allow Full Control, and click OK.

19. Click OK to close the Data (X:) Properties sheet.

20. Close the Windows Explorer window.

21. Click Start, and then click All Programs > Accessories > WordPad. A WordPad window appears.

22. Enter some text in the WordPad window.

23. Click File > Save As.

24. Save the file to the root of the X: drive, giving it the name **backuptest**.

25. Close the WordPad window.

26. Leave the computer logged on for the next exercise.

Exercise 9.1.3	Performing a Single Backup
Overview	In this exercise, you perform a single backup of your computer to the backup volume you created in Exercise 9.1.2.
Completion time	15 minutes

1. Click Start, and then click Administrative Tools > Windows Server Backup. Click Continue in the User Account Control message box, and the Windows Server Backup console appears, as shown in Figure 9-1-3.

Figure 9-1-3
Windows Server Backup console

2. In the actions pane, click Backup Once. The Backup Once Wizard appears, displaying the *Backup options* page.

3. Leave the Different options option selected, and click Next. The *Select backup configuration* page appears.

4. Select the Custom option, and click Next. The *Select backup items* page appears.

5. Select all of the volumes on the computer except the Backup (Z:) volume you created in Exercise 9.1.2.

6. Leave the Enable system recovery checkbox selected, and click Next. The *Specify destination type* page appears.

7. Leave the Local drives option selected, and click Next. The *Select backup destination* page appears.

8. In the Backup destination drop-down list, select Backup (Z:), and click Next. The *Specify advanced option* page appears.

9. Click Next to accept the default settings. The *Confirmation* page appears.

10. Click Backup. The *Backup progress* page appears and the backup begins.

11. When the backup is completed, press Ctrl+Prt Scr to take a screen shot of the *Backup progress* page, and then press Ctrl+V to paste the resulting image into the lab09_1_worksheet file in the page provided.

12. Click Close.

Question 1	What was the result of the backup job?

13. Leave the Windows Server Backup console open for the next exercise.

Exercise 9.1.4	Running an Incremental Backup
Overview	In this exercise, you perform a single backup of your computer to the backup volume you created in Exercise 9.1.2.
Completion time	20 minutes

1. In the Windows Server Backup console, in the Status area under Last Backup, click View details. The Details - Last Backup dialog box appears, as shown in Figure 9-1-4.

Figure 9-1-4

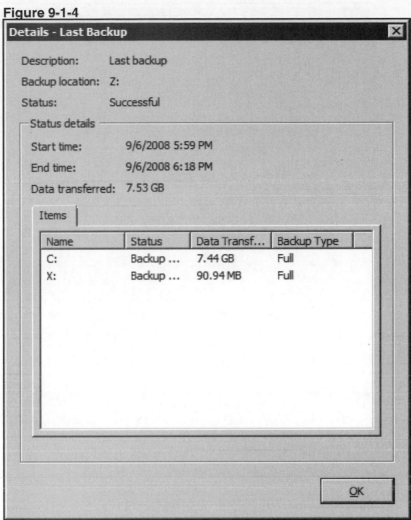

Details - Last Backup dialog box

2. In your worksheet, fill out Table 9-1-1 by using the information from the Details - Last Backup dialog box.

Table 9-1-1
Exercise 9.1.3 Backup Details

Drive	Data Transferred	Backup Type
C:	6.75 ~~PBg~~ GB	full
X:	78.81 MB	full

3. Click OK to close the Details - Last Backup dialog box.

4. In the actions pane, click Configure Performance Settings. The Optimize Backup Performance dialog box appears, as shown in Figure 9-1-5.

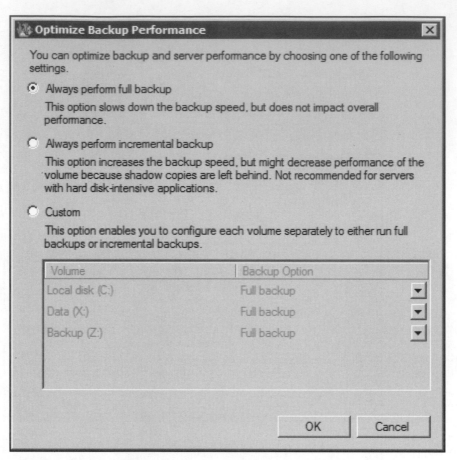

Figure 9-1-5
Optimize Backup Performance dialog box

5. Select the Always perform incremental backup option, and click OK.

6. Click Start, and then click All Programs > Accessories > Windows Explorer. A Windows Explorer window appears.

7. Browse to the C:\Windows folder, and double-click the WindowsUpdate text document file. A Notepad window appears, containing the contents of the file.

8. Key your name into the top line of the file, and click File > Save As.

9. Save the file to the Users\Student##\Documents folder, where ## is the number assigned to your computer.

10. Browse to the Data (X:) volume, and double-click the backuptest file you created in Exercise 9.1.2. The file opens in a WordPad window.

11. Modify the text in the file, and click File > Save.

12. Close the WordPad window.

13. Click Start, and then click All Programs > Accessories.

14. Right-click Command Prompt and, from the context menu, select Run as Administrator. Click Continue in the User Account Control message box, and a Command Prompt window appears.

15. In your worksheet, write out a command using the Wbadmin.exe program to execute a backup, using the same parameters you specified graphically in Exercise 9.1.3.

16. Key your command in the Command Prompt window, and press Enter. The backup begins.

17. When the backup is completed, press Ctrl+Prt Scr to take a screen shot of the Windows Server Backup console, showing the successful results, and then press Ctrl+V to paste the resulting image into the lab09_1_worksheet file in the page provided.

18. In the Windows Server Backup console, in the Status area under Last Backup, click View details. The Details - Last Backup dialog box appears.

Question 2	Did you just perform a full or an incremental backup from the Command Prompt?

19. Repeat steps 2 to 10 from Exercise 9.1.3 to run another single backup, using the same parameters.

20. Open the Details - Last Backup dialog box.

21. In your worksheet, fill out Table 9-1-2 by using the information from the Details - Last Backup dialog box.

Table 9-1-2
Exercise 9.1.4 Backup Details

Drive	Data Transferred	Backup Type
C:		
X:		

22. Click OK to close the Details - Last Backup dialog box.

23. Leave the Windows Server Backup console open for the next exercise.

Exercise 9.1.5	Recovering Data
Overview	In this exercise, you perform a single backup of your computer to the backup volume you created in Exercise 9.1.2.
Completion time	15 minutes

1. In the Windows Server Backup console in the actions pane, click Recover. The Recovery Wizard appears, displaying the *Getting started* page, as shown in Figure 9-1-6.

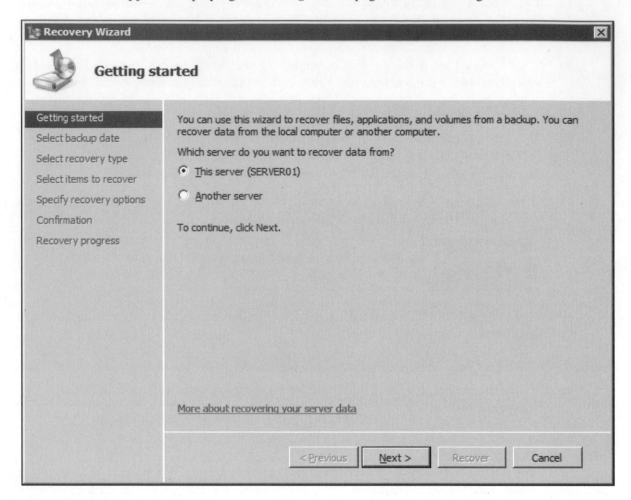

Figure 9-1-6
Recovery Wizard

2. Click Next to accept the default This server setting. The *Select backup date* page appears.

3. With today's date selected in the calendar, expand the Time drop-down list.

Question 3	*How many times appear in the drop-down list? What do they represent?*

4. Select the most recent time in the drop-down list, and click Next. The *Select recovery type* page appears.

5. Leave the Files and folders option selected, and click Next. The *Select items to recover* page appears.

6. In the Available items list, expand the Server## and Local disk (C:) folders, and select the Users folder. The contents of the Users folder appears.

7. With the contents of the Users folder selected, click Next. A Windows Server Backup message box appears, warning that you cannot recover the selected files to their original locations.

8. Click OK to continue. The *Specify recovery options* page appears.

9. In the Recovery destination box, click Browse. The Browse For Folder dialog box appears.

10. Browse to the Data (X:) volume, and click Make New Folder.

11. Give the new folder the name **Recovered Data**, and click OK. The path to the new folder appears in the Another location text box.

12. Click Next. The *Confirmation* page appears.

13. Click Recover. The Recovery progress window appears, and the recovery job starts.

14. When the recovery is complete, click Close.

15. Press Ctrl+Prt Scr to take a screen shot of the Windows Server Backup console, showing the successful result of the recovery job, and then press Ctrl+V to paste the resulting image into the lab09_1_worksheet file in the page provided.

16. In the console's Messages area, double-click the file recovery job you just performed. A File recovery dialog box appears.

Question 4	How much data was transferred during the recovery job?

Question 5	How can you explain the amount of data that was transferred during the recovery job compared with the amount of data transferred during the incremental backup job from which you are recovering data, as shown in Table 9-1-2?

17. Click OK to close the File recovery dialog box.

18. Close the Windows Server Backup console.

19. Log off of the computer.

LAB REVIEW QUESTIONS

Completion time	10 minutes

1. In Exercise 9.1.3, why can't you use the Full server option when performing the backup?

2. In Exercise 9.1.4, why was it necessary to open the Command Prompt window using the Run As Administrator command?

3. In Exercise 9.1.4, why did the Wbadmin.exe program perform a full backup of the C: drive, while in the second job you ran from the console, the C: backup was incremental?

4. In Exercise 9.1.5, what would happen if you cleared the Restore security settings checkbox on the *Specify recovery options* page of the Recovery Wizard?

LAB CHALLENGE: SCHEDULING A BACKUP JOB

Completion time	10 minutes

In addition to single, manual backups, Windows Server Backup is also capable of scheduling backups to occur every day or several times a day. To complete this challenge, you must create a scheduled job that backs up your Logical disk (C:) and Data (X:) volumes to the Backup (Z:) volume every two hours. List the steps you used to perform the procedure. After the backup runs, press Ctrl+Prt Scr to take a screen shot of the Windows Server Backup console, showing the job you created, and then press Ctrl+V to paste the resulting image into the lab09_1_worksheet file in the page provided.

LAB 10.1
DEPLOYING APPLICATIONS

This lab contains the following exercises and activities:

BEFORE YOU BEGIN

The classroom network consists of Windows Server 2008 student servers that are all connected to a local area network. There is also a classroom server, named ServerDC, that is connected to the same classroom network. ServerDC is also running Windows Server 2008 and is the domain controller for a domain named contoso.com. Throughout the labs in this manual, you will be working with the same student server on which you will install, configure, maintain, and troubleshoot application roles, features, and services.

Your instructor should have supplied you with the information needed to fill in the following table:

Student computer name (Server##)	
Student account name (Student##)	

To complete the exercises in this lab, you will require access to a second student computer on the classroom network, referred to in the exercises as your *partner server*. Depending on the configuration of your network, use one of the following options as directed by your instructor:

- For a conventional classroom network with one operating system installed on each computer, you must have a lab partner with his or her own computer, performing the same exercises as yourself.

- For a classroom in which each computer uses local virtualization software to install multiple operating systems, you must run two virtual machines representing student computers and perform the exercises separately on each virtual machine.

- For a classroom that uses online virtualization, you will have access to two virtual student servers in your Web browser. You must perform the exercises separately on each virtual machine.

Working with Lab Worksheets

Each lab in this manual requires that you answer questions, shoot screen shots, or perform other activities that you are to document in a worksheet named for the lab, such as lab01_worksheet. Your instructor will supply you with the worksheet files by copying them to the Students\Worksheets share on ServerDC. As you perform the exercises in each lab, open the appropriate worksheet file using WordPad, fill in the required information, and save the file to your computer's Student##\Documents folder. This folder is automatically redirected to the ServerDC computer. Your instructor will examine these worksheet files to assess your performance.

The procedure for opening and saving a worksheet file is as follows:

1. Click Start, and then click Run. The Run dialog box appears.

2. In the Open text box, key **\\ServerDC\Students\Worksheets\lab##_worksheet** (where lab## contains the number of the lab you're completing), and click OK.

3. The worksheet document opens in Wordpad.

4. Complete all of the exercises in the worksheet.

5. In WordPad, choose Save As from the File menu. The Save As dialog box appears.

6. In the File Name text box, key **lab##_worksheet_yourname** (where lab## contains the number of the lab you're completing and *yourname* is your last name), and click Save.

SCENARIO

You are an administrator for Contoso, Ltd., assigned to the test lab. Your supervisor wants to investigate various methods of deploying applications on network computers other than performing individual, manual installation. Toward this end, you begin exploring the capabilities of the Terminal Services role included with Windows Server 2008.

After completing this lab, you will be able to:

■ Install the Terminal Services role

■ Configure the Remote Desktop Connection client

■ Deploy RemoteApp applications

Estimated lab time: 130 minutes

Exercise 10.1.1	Installing the Terminal Services Role
Overview	For Windows Server 2008 to function as a terminal server, you must first install the Terminal Services role. In this exercise, you add the role with the Terminal Server role service, enabling the server to provide basic Terminal Services functionality.
Completion time	10 minutes

1. Turn on your computer. When the logon screen appears, log on using your Student## account and the password *P@ssw0rd*.

2. Close the Initial Configuration Tasks window when it appears.

3. Click Start, point to Administrative Tools, and click Server Manager. Click Continue in the User Account Control message box, and the Server Manager console appears.

4. Select the Roles node, and click Add Roles. The Add Roles Wizard appears, displaying the *Before You Begin* page.

5. Click Next to continue. The *Select Server Roles* page appears.

> **NOTE**
>
> *If your computer already has other roles or features installed, remove them before you proceed with this lab.*

6. Select the Terminal Services role, and click Next. The *Introduction to Terminal Services* page appears.

7. Click Next to bypass the introductory page. The *Select Role Services* page appears, as shown in Figure 10-1-1.

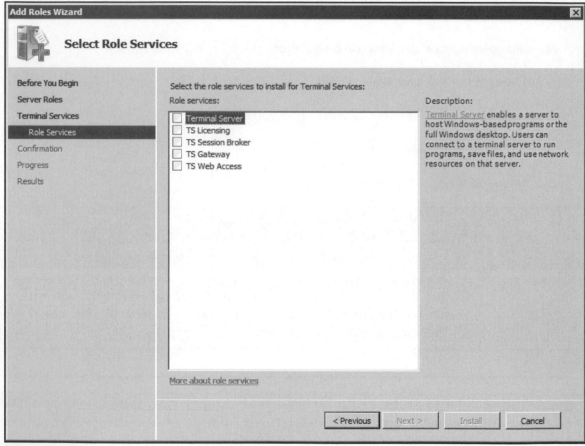

Figure 10-1-1
Select Role Services page of the Add Roles Wizard

8. Select the Terminal Server role service, and click Next. The *Uninstall and Reinstall Applications for Compatibility* page appears.

9. Click Next to continue. The *Specify Authentication Method for Terminal Server* page appears.

10. Select the Do not require Network Level Authentication option, and click Next. The *Specify Licensing Mode* page appears.

11. Select the Configure Later option, and click Next. The *Select User Groups Allowed Access To This Terminal Server* page appears.

12. Click Add. The Select Users, Computers, or Groups dialog box appears.

13. In the Enter Object Names to Select box, key **Students**, and click OK.

14. Press Ctrl+Prt Scr to take a screen shot of the *Select User Groups Allowed Access To This Terminal Server* page, and then press Ctrl+V to paste the resulting image into the lab10_1_worksheet file in the page provided.

15. Click Next to accept the specified groups. The *Confirm Installation Selections* page appears.

16. Click Install. The wizard installs the role, and the *Installation Results* page appears.

17. Click Close. An Add Roles Wizard message box appears, prompting you to restart the computer.

18. Click Yes. The computer restarts.

19. When the logon screen appears, log on using your Student## account and the password *P@ssw0rd*. Server Manager loads and completes the role installation.

20. Click Close to close the Resume Configuration Wizard.

21. Close Server Manager, and leave the computer logged on for the next exercise.

Exercise 10.1.2	Configuring the Remote Desktop Connection Client
Overview	In this exercise, you configure the Remote Desktop Connection client, preparing it to connect to a terminal server.
Completion time	10 minutes

1. Click Start, and then click All Programs > Accessories > Notepad. A Notepad window appears.

2. Key some text in the Notepad window, and then click File > Save As. The Save As combo box appears.

3. Save the text file to your Documents folder, using the name **Lab10**.

4. Close the Notepad window.

5. Click Start, and then click All Programs > Accessories > Remote Desktop Connection. The Remote Desktop Connection dialog box appears.

6. Click Options. The dialog box expands, as shown in Figure 10-1-2.

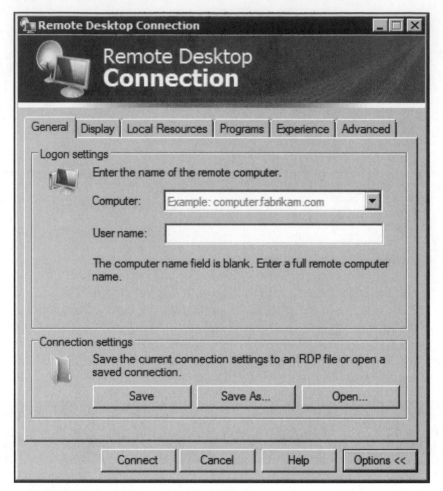

Figure 10-1-2
Remote Desktop Connection dialog box

7. Click the Display tab.

8. In the Remote Desktop Size box, use the slider to select a resolution just below that of your current display.

9. Click the Local Resources tab.

10. In the Remote Computer Sound box, select Do Not Play from the drop-down list.

11. In the Local Devices and Resources box, clear the Printers checkbox, and leave the Clipboard checkbox selected.

12. Click the Experience tab.

13. In the Performance drop-down list, select LAN (10 Mbps Or Higher).

14. Click the General tab.

15. Leave the Remote Desktop Connection window open for the next exercise.

Exercise 10.1.3	Establishing a Terminal Services Connection
Overview	In this exercise, you use the Remote Desktop Connection client to initiate a Terminal Services connection to your partner server.
Completion time	10 minutes

NOTE	*Before you initiate the connection to your partner server, make sure that Exercise 10.1.1 has been completed on that computer and that it is ready to receive remote connections.*

1. In the Remote Desktop Connection client program, on the General tab, key **Server##** in the Computer text box, where ## is the number assigned to your partner server by your instructor.

2. In the User Name field, key **contoso\student##**, where ## is the number assigned to your computer.

3. Click Connect. A Windows Security dialog box appears.

4. Under the contoso\student## user name, key **P@ssw0rd**, and click OK. A Server## - Remote Desktop window appears, containing the Initial Configuration Tasks window.

5. Close the Initial Configuration Tasks window.

6. In the Server## - Remote Desktop window, click Start, and then click All Programs > Accessories > Notepad. A Notepad window appears.

Question 1	*On which computer is the Notepad application actually running?*

7. Click File > Open. The Open combo box appears.

8. Press Ctrl+Prt Scr to take a screen shot of the Server## - Remote Desktop window, showing the Open combo box, and then press Ctrl+V to paste the resulting image into the lab10_1_worksheet file in the page provided.

Question 2	On which computer is the user profile stored that appears within the Student## folder (where ## is the number assigned to your computer)?

9. Select the Lab10 text file you created at the beginning of this exercise, and click Open.

10. Modify the text in the file, and save it.

11. Leave the Notepad window open, and click the Close button in the title bar of the Server## - Remote Desktop window. A Disconnect Terminal Services Session message box appears, asking whether you want to disconnect.

12. Click OK. The RDC client disconnects from the terminal server.

Question 3	Is Notepad still running on your partner server? Explain why or why not.

13. Leave the computer logged on for the next exercise.

Exercise 10.1.4	Creating an RDP File
Overview	In this exercise, you use the RDC client to create an RDP file, which you can use to connect to a specific terminal server using a predetermined collection of configuration settings.
Completion time	10 minutes

1. Click Start, and then click All Programs > Accessories > Remote Desktop Connection. The Remote Desktop Connection dialog box appears.

2. Click Options. The dialog box expands.

3. In the Connection Settings box, click Save As. The Save As combo box appears.

4. Click Browse Folders. The combo box expands, as shown in Figure 10-1-3.

5. In the left pane, click Desktop.

6. In the File Name text box, key **Server##**, where ## is the number assigned to your partner server.

7. Click Save. A Server## icon appears on your desktop.

8. Click the Display tab.

9. In the Remote Desktop Size box, set the slider to Full Screen.

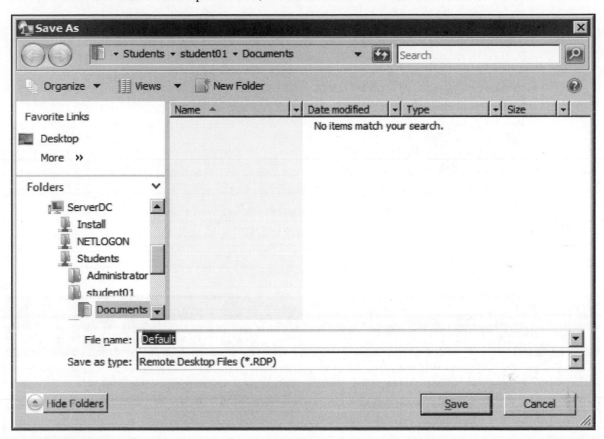

Figure 10-1-3
Save As combo box

10. Click Connect. A Remote Desktop Connection message box appears, asking whether you trust the remote connection.

11. Click Connect. The Windows Security dialog box appears.

12. Log on using the password *P@ssw0rd*, and click OK. The RDC client connects to the terminal server and the desktop appears, with the Notepad window you opened in Exercise 10.1.2 still open.

Question 4	Is the taskbar at the bottom of your screen being generated by your server or your partner server? How can you tell?

13. Click the Close button in the connection bar to disconnect from the terminal server session.

14. Press Ctrl+Prt Scr to take a screen shot of your server's desktop, showing the Server## RDP icon, and then press Ctrl+V to paste the resulting image into the lab10_1_worksheet file in the page provided.

15. Double-click the Server## icon. A Remote Desktop Connection message box appears, warning you that the publisher of the remote connection cannot be identified.

16. Click Connect, log on using the password *P@ssw0rd*, and click OK. The RDC client connects to the terminal server.

17. In the remote session window, click Start. Click the arrow button and, on the context menu, click Log Off.

Question 5	What happens?

Question 6	*Is the Notepad application you opened in Exercise 4.2 still open in the terminal server session? Why or why not?*

18. Leave the computer logged on for the next exercise.

Exercise 10.1.5	**Configuring RemoteApp Applications**
Overview	In this exercise, you configure your terminal server to deploy individual applications using RemoteApp.
Completion time	10 minutes

1. Click Start, and then click Administrative Tools > Terminal Services > TS RemoteApp Manager. Click Continue in the User Account Control message box, and the TS RemoteApp Manager console appears, as shown in Figure 10-1-4.

2. In the actions pane, click Add RemoteApp Programs. The RemoteApp Wizard appears.

3. Click Next to bypass the Welcome page. The *Choose Programs To Add To The RemoteApp Programs List* page appears.

4. Select the WordPad checkbox, and click Properties. The RemoteApp Properties sheet for WordPad appears.

5. Clear the RemoteApp program is available through TS Web Access checkbox.

6. Select the Allow any command line arguments option, and click OK. A RemoteApp Wizard message box appears, warning you that allowing executable files to run with no restrictions on the command line arguments opens the terminal server to attack.

7. Click Yes.

8. Click Next. The *Review Settings* page appears.

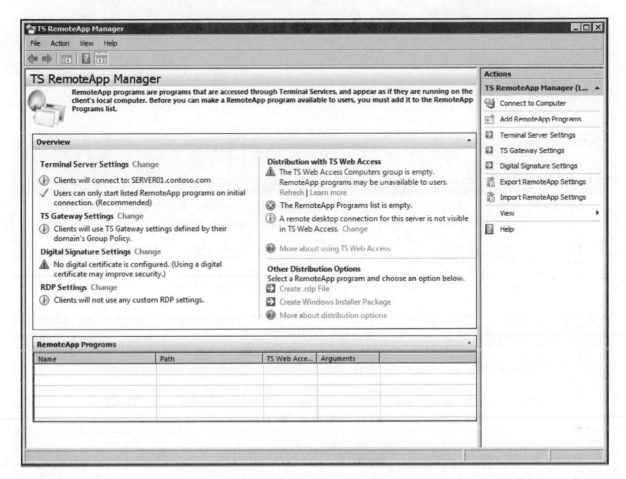

Figure 10-1-4
TS RemoteApp Manager console

9. Click Finish. The WordPad application appears in the RemoteApp Programs list.

10. Repeat steps 2 to 9 to add the Server Manager and System Information applications to the RemoteApp Programs list, clearing the RemoteApp program is available through TS Web Access checkbox and leaving the default Do not allow command line arguments setting for each.

11. Press Ctrl+Prt Scr to take a screen shot of the TS RemoteApp Manager console, showing the applications you added, and then press Ctrl+V to paste the resulting image into the lab10_1_worksheet file in the page provided.

Question 7	In the TS RemoteApp Manager console, there are currently two warning indicators showing in the Overview area. Will any of these warnings make it impossible to access your RemoteApp applications from your partner server? Explain why or why not.

12. Leave the TS RemoteApp Manager console open for the next exercise.

Exercise 10.1.6	Creating RemoteApp RDP Files
Overview	In this exercise, you create RDP files that enable clients to access the RemoteApp applications you configured in Exercise 10.1.5.
Completion time	10 minutes

1. In the TS RemoteApp Manager console, in the RemoteApp Programs list, select the WordPad application you added in Exercise 10.1.5.

2. In the actions pane, select Create .rdp File. The RemoteApp Wizard appears.

3. Click Next to bypass the *Welcome to the RemoteApp Wizard* page. The *Specify Package Settings* page appears, as shown in Figure 10-1-5.

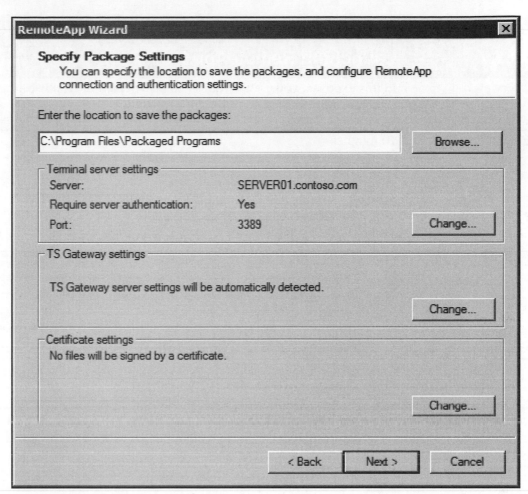

Figure 10-1-5
Specify Package Settings page of the RemoteApp Wizard

4. In the Enter the location to save the packages text box, key **\\serverdc\students\
    student##\documents**, where ## is the number assigned to your computer, and then
    click Next. The *Review Settings* page appears.

5. Click Finish. The wizard closes, and an RDP file named for the application appears in
    your Documents folder.

6. Repeat steps 2 to 5 to create an RDP file for the System Information application in your
    Documents folder.

7. Close the TS RemoteApp Manager console.

8. Log off of the computer.

Exercise 10.1.7	Launching RemoteApp RDP Files
Overview	In this exercise, you use the RDP files you created in Exercise 10.1.6 to establish terminal server connections from your partner server.
Completion time	10 minutes

1. Move to your partner server, and log on to the domain using your Student## account, where ## is the number assigned to your computer, and the password *P@ssw0rd*.

2. Click Start, and then click All Programs > Accessories > Windows Explorer. A Windows Explorer window appears, displaying the contents of your Documents folder.

Question 8	Why is your Documents folder accessible from your partner server?

3. In the Documents folder, double-click the WordPad RDP file. A RemoteApp message box appears, warning that the publisher of the remote connection cannot be identified.

4. Click Connect. A Windows Security dialog box appears.

5. Log on using your contoso\Student## account and the password *P@ssw0rd*. A WordPad window appears.

Question 9	On which computer is the Wordpad.exe file running?

6. In the WordPad window, click File > Open. The Open combo box appears.

7. Browse to the Local Disk (C:) drive.

Question 10	Are you looking at the Local Disk (C:) drive on your partner server or on your computer, the terminal server? How can you tell?

8. Click Cancel to close the Open combo box.

9. While still on your partner server, switch back to Windows Explorer, and double-click the Msinfo32 RDP file for the System Information application.

10. Click Connect to bypass the Unknown Publisher warning. The System Information window appears.

Question 11	For which computer does the System Information window contain information?

11. Close the Wordpad and System Information windows.

12. Log off of your partner computer.

Exercise 10.1.8	Creating Windows Installer Files
Overview	In this exercise, you create Windows Installer (.msi) package files that you can use to deploy your RemoteApp applications all over the network.
Completion time	10 minutes

1. Return to your own computer, and log on using your Student## account and the password *P@ssw0rd*.

2. Close the Initial Configuration Tasks window when it appears.

3. Open the TS RemoteApp Manager console and, in the RemoteApp Programs list, select the Server Manager application you added in Exercise 10.1.5.

4. In the actions pane, select Create Windows Installer Package. The RemoteApp Wizard appears.

5. Click Next to bypass the *Welcome to the RemoteApp Wizard* page. The *Specify Package Settings* page appears.

6. In the Enter the location to save the packages text box, key **\\serverdc\students\student##\documents**, where ## is the number assigned to your computer, and then click Next. The *Configure Distribution Package* page appears, as shown in Figure 10-1-6.

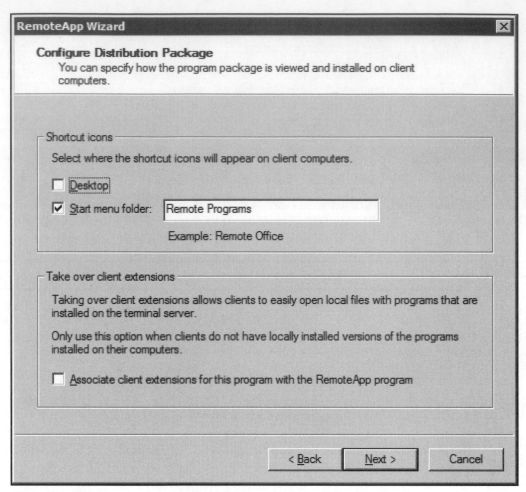

Figure 10-1-6
Configure Distribution Package page of the RemoteApp Wizard

7. In the Start menu folder text box, key **Server## Remote Programs**, where ## is the number assigned to your computer, and then click Next. The *Review Settings* page appears.

8. Click Finish. The wizard closes, and a Windows Installer file with the name CompMgmtLauncher appears in your Documents folder.

9. Close the TS RemoteApp Manager console.

10. Log off of the computer.

Exercise 10.1.9	**Running Windows Installer Files**
Overview	In this exercise, you move to your partner server and launch the Windows Installer package file you created in Exercise 10.1.8.
Completion time	10 minutes

1. Move to your partner server, and log on using your Student## account, where ## is the number assigned to your computer, and the password *P@ssw0rd*.

2. Open Windows Explorer. The contents of your Documents folder appear.

3. In the Documents folder, double-click the CompMgmtLauncher file.

4. If a Open File – Security Warning dialog box appears, click Run. A User Account Control dialog box appears.

5. Click Allow.

6. While still on your partner server, click Start, and then click All Programs > Server## Remote Programs > Server Manager. A RemoteApp message box appears, warning that the publisher of the remote connection cannot be identified.

7. Click Connect. A Windows Security dialog box appears.

8. Log on using your contoso\Student## account with the password *P@ssw0rd*. A Connected To Server##.contoso.com window appears, containing another User Account Control dialog box.

9. Press Ctrl+Prt Scr to take a screen shot of the Connected to SERVER##.contoso.com window, and then press Ctrl+V to paste the resulting image into the lab10_1_worksheet file in the page provided.

10. In the User Account Control dialog box, click Continue. The Server Manager console appears.

Question 12	*Why did two User Account Control dialog boxes appear during the terminal server connection sequence?*

11. Close the Server Manager console.

12. Log off of the computer.

LAB REVIEW QUESTIONS

Completion time	10 minutes

1. In Exercise 10.1.2, you created a Lab10 text file on your computer at the beginning of the exercise. Later, while working within a terminal server session on your partner server, you opened a file using Notepad and accessed the Documents folder in your user profile on that computer. Why does the Lab10 file appear in the Documents folder on your partner server when you originally created it on your own server?

2. In Exercises 10.1.4 and 10.1.7, you used the RDC client to connect to your partner server on two separate occasions, once interactively and once using the RDP file you created. How can you tell from this experience that the RDP file includes the settings you configured in the client before you created the RDP file?

3. In Exercise 10.1.7, you opened two separate RemoteApp applications on your computer using your partner server as the client. How many sessions did you open on the terminal server by launching these two applications? How can you tell?

LAB CHALLENGE: DEPLOYING REMOTEAPP APPLICATIONS USING GROUP POLICY

Completion time	20 minutes

Your supervisor wants to be able to deploy terminal server applications to users' desktops using RemoteApp and Group Policy, without the need for any configuration by the user. To complete this challenge, demonstrate that this is possible by deploying the Calculator program on your terminal server to all other computers in the classroom. As you proceed, be sure to observe the following restrictions.

-   Make sure your deployed application is properly identified on the users' desktops as Server## Calculator, where ## is the number assigned to your computer.

-   Do not modify any of the existing Group Policy objects in the Active Directory tree. Create your own GPO, naming it Student##, and link it as needed.

On your worksheet, list all of the tasks you must perform to complete this challenge.

WORKSTATION RESET: RETURNING TO BASELINE

Completion time	10 minutes

To return the computer to its baseline state, complete the following procedures.

1.   Open the Group Policy Management console, and unlink any GPOs you created during the course of the lab.

2.   Open the Server Manager console, and remove the Terminal Services role.

NOTES

NOTES

NOTES

NOTES

NOTES

NOTES

NOTES

NOTES

NOTES

NOTES

NOTES

NOTES

NOTES